All Around America

The Time Traveler's
Talk Show

D1606909

Eighteen Radio Scripts for Cooperative Oral Reading

Raymond C. Clark
Anne Siebert

PRO LINGUA ASSOCIATES

Pro Lingua Associates, Publishers
P.O. Box 1348
Brattleboro, Vermont 05302 USA
Office: 802 257 7779
Orders: 800 366 4775
E-mail: info@ProLinguaAssociates.com
WebStore www.ProLinguaAssociates.com
SAN: 216-0579

*At Pro Lingua
our objective is to foster an approach
to learning and teaching that we call
interplay, the **inter**action of language
learners and teachers with their materials,
with the language and culture,
and with each other in active, creative
and productive **play**.*

Copyright © 2004 by Raymond C. Clark and Anne Siebert

ISBN 0-86647-183-9

This book was designed by Arthur A. Burrows. The text was set in Bookman Oldstyle, a modern, bold adaptation of a traditional square serif face; it is an Agfa digital font. The cover display type is Trebuchet. The book was printed and bound by Boyd Printing Company in Albany, New York.

Illustrations in this book have come from the following sources: the National Archives; the Library of Congress; Museum of Fine Arts, Boston (portraits of Sam Adams and Paul Revere by John Singleton Copley and of Abigail Adams by Gilbert Stuart); the Lowell National Historic Park; the Thoreau Society (daguerreotype of Thoreau); the Records of U.S. Army Military History Institute National Archives (photo of Gen. Lee); Chicago Historical Society; Chicago buildings courtesy of the Francis Loeb Library, Graduate School of Design at Harvard, and Skidmore, Owings, and Merrill, LLP; Lemhi-Shoshone Sacajawea Birthplace site; the Governor's website for the State of Hawai'i - Washington Place; Sausalito Historical Society (photo of J.P. Strauss); 'Swift Arrow" National Archives Select List 146 by H.T. Corey 1916; "Running Deer" National Archives Select List 114 Paliwahtiwa, Governor of the Zuñi by Ben Wittick; University of Texas Intitute of Texas Culture, San Antonio; French Quarter by Gary's Photos and Buskers on Royal St. by John Coulthard; National Portrait Gallery, Smithsonian Institution (www.npg.si/edu photo of Louis Armstrong); Space Center photos courtesy of NASA; Castillo photos courtesy of National Park Service www.nps.gov; courtesy PBS (Maya Lin photo © 2003 art21/pbs); and of Art Explosion 750,000 Images™ (© 2000 Nova Development Corporation); The Big Box of Art™ (© 2001 Hermera Technologies, Inc.™); and personal photos.

Printed in the United States of America
First printing 2004. 2000 copies.

ABOUT THE COVER

J D Rivera, the talk show host of *All Around America,* is a fictitious character who has traveled extensively all around Planet Earth throughout history.

Liliuokalani, the last Queen of Hawaii, was a real person. This image from the cover is a composite picture based on a photograph taken of Lydia Liliuokalani as queen (1891-1894) and a 2004 photo of her living room in the home she called Washington Place. She was a musician and composer, and this piano on which she wrote the ever popular *Aloha 'Oe* was her most prized possession.

After Liliuokalani's death in 1917, Washington Place was the Governors' Mansion for the State of Hawaii until 2001 when Governor Linda Lingle restored it to the people of Hawaii as a museum. *Photos copyright © 2003-4 State of Hawai`i*

The photos on the back cover are of the Golden Gate Bridge in San Francisco, the U.S. Capitol Building in Washington, D.C., the Statue of Liberty in New York Harbor, the Vietnam Memorial in Washington, D.C., Mount Rushmore in South Dakota, the Grand Canyon of the Colorado in Arizona, and the statue of Hawaiian King Kamehameha I on the island of Oahu.

Visiting Sites All Around America

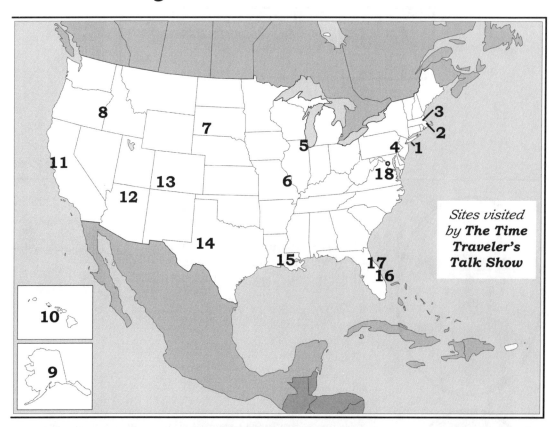

Sites visited
by **The Time
Traveler's
Talk Show**

Contents

Introduction

All Around America, The Time Traveler's Talk Show and its companion ***Study Guide*** is an intermediate-advanced level program for English language learners. This book is a dramatic reader which the learners use as a cooperative reading experience. The eighteen units (shows) explore the history, culture, and nature of the United States and provide opportunities to develop English language skills.

The text is based on the format of a radio talk show. There are a host, a local personality (often a guide), famous and imaginary personalities from the past, and callers and emailers from cities around the U.S. The language used by the participants is informal, educated conversational English, similar to what would be heard on local or national talk shows. Consequently, the language is idiomatic. By working with the talk show format, the learners will be enabled to continue their learning on their own by listening to real talk shows. They should be encouraged to listen to talk shows on National Public Radio.

The eighteen radio scripts are also available in a two-CD format for listening practice. Although use of the CDs is certainly optional, the CDs may be used a in a variety of ways to enhance the learning experience.

The show moves from place to place, around the United States, and with each stop, there is considerable description of what is there and what happened there. For that reason, the text contains over 200 adjectives. As the learners work through the text, they will encounter natural recycling of the adjectives, and also re-occurences of nouns and verbs. For that reason it is best to begin with the first unit (The Statue of Liberty) and proceed through the book unit by unit to the end (Washington, D.C.).

The text and the study guide can be used in a variety of ways. The recommended procedure is as follows:

1. **Begin with the Study Guide**. Introduce the locale and engage the students in an initial discussion:
    Where is the Statue of Liberty?
    What does it look like?
    Has anybody seen it?

Introduction

2. **Do Parts A and B in the Study Guide** (See the introduction to the Study Guide for additional suggestions). This prepares the learners for the content of the talk show. Notice that there is emphasis on the nouns which are critical to understanding the show.

3. **Do Part C in the Study Guide**. This exercise is basically a matching exercise that prepares the learners for the idioms and expressions they will encounter in the talk show. Answers are provided in the back of the Study Guide.

4. **Do the talk show**. This can be done in a variety of ways. One procedure would be:

    A. **Assign parts and have the learners read their lines aloud**. Stop for questions and answers as the class works carefully through the lines. Note and fix pronunciation problems.

    B. **Read through the script again**. This time with more expressiveness and fluency.

    C. **Use the Fact Sheets**. At the end of each show, the host asks for additional callers to call in with questions. In the back of the book, there are Fact Sheets for each show. Learners who do not have parts or very brief parts, use the facts to ask one of the performers a question (the teacher can also participate). This is practicing question formation. The learners can be encouraged to ad lib and play with the manner in which they ask the questions. For example:

       Fact #1:   The Statue of Liberty is located on Liberty Island.

       Learner A: *I'd like to ask Billie Jefferson a question. Where is the Statue of Liberty located?*
       Learner B (Jefferson): *I'm glad you asked. It's located on Liberty Island.*
       Learner A: *And where is Liberty Island?*
       Learner B: *In New York Harbor.*

    D. **Do a final, dramatic reading, record it, and play it back.**

5. **Return to the Study Guide and do the True-False Review.** This simple activity reviews the show and checks comprehension. The answers are in the back.

Introduction

6. **Do Exercise E. Vocabulary Review.**

7. **Do Exercise F.** This is a summary of the adjectives used in the show. It can be used in a variety of ways.

8. **Do Exercise G.** This is an opportunity to practice writing on a topic that relates to the show.

9. **Assign Exercise H**. Encourage the learners to go to the web and explore the topic in greater detail. They can report on their virtual visit the next time the class meets.

The CD's provide an additional dimension to the learning experience. Although the CDs are certainly optional, and not necessarily central to the purpose of the text and Study Guide, they can be used in a number of ways.

1. **Play the entire appropriate track on the CD**. After doing Step 1, above (introducing the site), play the track once through without stopping to allow the learners to practice their global listening comprehension skills.

2. **Follow up with an informal question and answer session**, asking who, what, where, when, how, and why questions.

3. After doing exercises A, B, and C in the Study Guide, **play the show as the learners follow along in the text.** Alternatively, this can be done before the learners begin to read the text. You can play it straight through without stopping, or, if the learners are having difficulty, stop after every two or three characters have spoken several lines and check for comprehension with questions, or allow the learners to ask questions.

4. After the learners have recorded their own program, **play the entire show** to allow the learners to compare pronunciation, phrasing, and dramatics.

5. **Make the CD available in a language lab** to allow the learners to study on their own.

Note: *The track numbers on CD 1 correspond to the show numbers 1 to 9 in the table of contents; see page v. On CD 2, shows 10 to 18 are listed on the label, but your CD player will register them as tracks 1-9.*

The Statue of Liberty
A Beacon of Freedom

"Lady Liberty"

The Statue of Liberty is a symbol of freedom. It is in New York Harbor. It is known all over the world. It is a statue of a woman holding a torch. She was a gift from France to celebrate friendship and America's 100th anniversary. She is a beloved symbol, especially for immigrants who came to America for a better life.

Billie

Time Travelers

J D Rivera, Talk Show Host
Billie Jefferson, Guide
Frederic Auguste Bartholdi, Sculptor
Alexandre Gustave Eiffel, Engineer
Joseph Pulitzer, Publisher
Caller from Cleveland, Ohio
Caller from Trenton, New Jersey

The Statue of Liberty

Gustave Eiffel

Frederic Auguste
Bartholdi

Joseph Pulitzer

Rivera Welcome to *All Around America: The Time Traveler's Talk Show,* a timeless program that takes you to famous places all around America where you'll meet the people who made history. This is your host, J D Rivera, talking to you from our mobile studio. Today for our very first program we're at the base of one of America's most famous symbols, the Statue of Liberty — so American, yet born in France. With me is Billie Jefferson, one of the guides here at the statue. Welcome Billie.

Jefferson Thank you, and welcome to Liberty Island and the Statue of Liberty National Monument.

Rivera OK, Billie. Now, tell us a little about Lady Liberty.

Jefferson Well, as you know, this is one of America's great symbols. She stands for freedom, an idea so near and dear to all Americans – actually to people around the world. As you mentioned, our beautiful lady came here from France. She was created by a great French sculptor, Frederic Bartholdi.

Rivera   And on the line with us from Paris, France is Mr. Frederic Bartholdi. Mr. Bartholdi, welcome to our show. It's great to have you with us.

Bartholdi   Thank you, J D. It's good to be here.

Rivera   So, Mr. Bartholdi, in the first place, why did you make Lady Liberty?

Bartholdi   Bien, America's one hundredth birthday was coming up, so in France the idea of a gift was on our minds. You know, of course, that France and America have always had a special friendship. A friend of mine suggested that the gift should be something that would symbolize an idea both countries love — liberty. And, voila! The Statue of Liberty was born.

Rivera   And how long did it take to give birth to Lady Liberty, and was it a long, hard labor?

Bartholdi   Ha! Actually, it took over ten years, much longer than I'd expected.We ran out of money several times, so construction had to be stopped. And yes, it was hard to do. Because the statue is so huge, one of the biggest problems was getting the statue to stand up. Without Mr. Alexander Eiffel, I couldn't have done it.

Rivera   And I think we have Mr. Eiffel on the line. Mr. Eiffel, are you there?

Eiffel   Yes, I am. Thanks for letting me be on your show. It was a great pleasure to help with the statue. I designed the framework, the internal structure, so Lady Liberty could stand. It was important that winds or storms would not knock her down. It was a real challenge.

The Statue of Liberty

Jefferson Excuse me, Mr. Eiffel, but you must be the person who created the Eiffel Tower, aren't you?

Eiffel Yes, I am proud to say that I did that, as well as many other constructions.

Rivera Thanks so much to the two of you. We owe you a lot.

Bartholdi My pleasure, J D.

Eiffel And mine.

Rivera And now, Billie, I have an email question here from Denver, Colorado, that asks us to tell about the role Mr. Joseph Pulitzer played.

Jefferson Well, after the statue was made, there was no money left to build a pedestal. The statue needed a platform to stand on, and...

Pulitzer Hello, J D and Billie. I think you wanted me to join you.

Rivera Mr. Joseph Pulitzer. What a pleasure! Tell us what you did.

Pulitzer The statue was finished, but she had nothing to stand on. I am proud to say that my newspaper, *The New York World,* was able to raise thousands of dollars to pay for the pedestal. We asked people from across America to send in whatever they could. Even school children sent in their nickels and dimes so that Lady Liberty would not be without a pedestal. The whole nation responded. It was inspiring!

Jefferson You were deeply interested in this project, weren't you, sir?

Pulitzer Yes, I was. After all, I was an immigrant. I came from Hungary, and the idea of freedom that the statue symbolized was very important to me. I think sometimes Americans born here take freedom for granted.

Rivera   How true! And by the way, Mr. Pulitzer, are you the Joseph Pulitzer who established the Pulitzer Prizes for outstanding achievement in letters?

Pulitzer   One and the same, J D. I established it in 1917.

Rivera   Thanks for being on the show Mr. Pulitzer. Like so many immigrants, your contributions have meant so much to this country. And, I believe we have a caller from Cleveland, Ohio, on the line. Go ahead, Cleveland.

Cleveland   Hello, J D and Billie. My name is Hannah Steinberg. I saw this wonderful lady when I sailed into New York Harbor in 1939 with my husband. We were escaping a terrible situation in Europe as World War II was starting. So when I saw her, I cried. It was so hard to leave our lives in Europe, but we were so happy to be safe and free.

Rivera   After the war, did you go back to Europe?

Cleveland   No. We became U.S. citizens, and although we have gone back for a visit, this is our home now, and we are so thankful that America took us in. We hope the doors will always be open, and we hope Lady Liberty's words will always welcome the tired, the poor, and the homeless. Thanks for taking my call.

Rivera   And thank you. Billie, perhaps you can explain what she meant by "Lady Liberty's words."

Jefferson   She was referring to the poem by Emma Lazarus at the base of the statue. It goes like this: "Give me your tired, your poor, Your huddled masses yearning to breathe free . . . Send these the homeless tempest-tost to me"

Rivera   And we have another call. This time from Trenton, New Jersey. Welcome to the show.

The Statue of Liberty

Trenton   Thank you. I am Amra, and I am so happy to be on your show. Ten years ago I came from Bosnia, and I could not speak English. Now I am on your show! I want to tell everybody that I did not see the statue when I arrived on the plane, but I have visited New York many times, and I have seen her in person. She is still wonderful to me.

Jefferson   Have you been to the island and gone inside?

Trenton   Absolutely! I climbed all the way to the crown. Every step! You can see New York. It is a wonderful view.

Rivera   Thank you so much, Amra. Lady Liberty is indeed quite a sight.

Jefferson   And you should see her at night. The torch shines all night. She is truly a beacon of freedom that has greeted millions of immigrants on their way to Ellis Island.

Rivera   Before we go, Billie, tell us a little about Ellis Island.

Jefferson   Ellis Island is in the harbor right next to us. It's the place where millions of immigrants arriving in New York were processed and admitted to the U.S. Now, it's the Ellis Island Immigration Museum and part of the Statue of Liberty National Monument.

Rivera   So, folks, there you have it. Our first stop at one of America's treasures, the Statue of Liberty. And don't forget to tune in next week when we'll be in Boston, Massachusetts, but before we go there's still time for our listeners to call in with comments and questions.

The Boston Freedom Trail

A Walk in Revolutionary America

Boston Massacre 1770

Faneuil Hall 2004

The Freedom Trail is a 2.5 mile walking tour in downtown Boston. Boston is where the American Revolution began. Some of the important events were the Boston Massacre, the Boston Tea Party, Paul Revere's Ride and the Battle of Bunker Hill.

Chris

Time Travelers

J D Rivera, Talk Show Host
Chris Ryan, Park Guide
Abigail Adams, Writer, Wife of John Adams
Samuel Adams, Patriot
Paul Revere, Patriot
Caller from Detroit, Michigan
Caller from Seattle, Washington

The Boston Freedom Trail

Paul Revere

Abigail Adams

Sam Adams

Rivera   Good morning. This is J D Rivera, your host for *All Around America, The Time Traveler's Talk Show.* Today we are in the city of Boston, Massachusetts. After visiting Lady Liberty, it is appropriate to be in Boston where, in the 1770s, the words "liberty" and "freedom" began to be heard daily in meeting places like Faneuil Hall, and on the streets and in the city's central park, The Boston Common. We are at the beginning of The Freedom Trail with our guide for today, Chris Ryan. Hello Chris.

Ryan   Hello, J D. Welcome to the Freedom Trail. It's a two and a half mile walk along the streets of Boston. You just follow the red line on the sidewalk and you'll pass by 16 historic sites in just a couple of hours.

Rivera   A couple of hours is out of the question for our program, so why don't you tell us about some of the highlights.

Ryan   I'd be glad to. Let's begin with the site of the Boston Massacre.

Rivera   John Adams was involved with that, and I asked him to be here today, but he couldn't make it, so filling in for him is John's better half, his wife Abigail Adams. Mrs. Adams, you yourself are well-known as a great letter writer, recording the events of those early years. Mrs. Adams, what can you tell us about the Boston Massacre?

A. Adams It happened in March, 1770, just in front of the Customs House. People were rather upset about the heavy taxes imposed by the British government and an angry mob confronted a group of soldiers — we called them Redcoats, and they were not very popular. In a panic, the soldiers fired at the crowd.

Rivera And so what happened?

A. Adams Five people were killed.

Rivera Excuse me, Mrs. Adams, but we have a caller on the line with a question. Hello, Detroit, what's your question?

Detroit Mrs. Adams, I know your husband was a leader of the American Revolution, but I read that he defended the British soldiers in court.

A. Adams That's true he did. He felt it was his duty to defend them. He was a skilled lawyer, and he felt the rule of law must be more important than mob rule.

Detroit And he won, didn't he?

A. Adams He did, and I'm sure he would do it all over again, even though he was a strong advocate of the rights of the American colonials.

Rivera Thank you very much, Mrs. Adams. Your husband went on to do great things for his country: patriot, diplomat, vice-president, and second president of the U.S., and your son John Quincy Adams followed in his father's footsteps and became the sixth president of the U.S.

Detroit I have another question, J D.

Rivera Go ahead.

Detroit   I've read that the leader of the Boston mob was Crispus Attucks, an African American, Is that true?

Rivera   Will you take that, Chris?

Ryan   Sure. Crispus Attucks was the child of an African American slave and an Indian mother. Attucks himself was born a slave, but he ran away and probably spent some years at sea. He later returned to Boston and joined the angry mob that confronted the Redcoats. He was the first man to die for America's freedom.

Rivera   How ironic! Thanks for your call, Detroit.

Ryan   Now, J D, let me take you to another important scene of the American Revolution. Actually, it's not on the trail. It's in the water, in Boston Harbor. And there the angry Bostonians had a tea party.

Rivera   A tea party? That doesn't sound like a very revolutionary thing to do.

S. Adams   J D and Chris, I've been standing by and I'd like to jump in here.

Rivera   Of course. This is Mr. Samuel Adams. Go ahead Mr. Adams.

S. Adams   I organized that party because we Bostonians were sick and tired of the taxes King George wanted us to pay.

Rivera   And so you had a party?

S. Adams   Damned right! A group of us dressed up like Indians, boarded some British ships and threw a few hundred boxes of tea into the water in protest over taxation without representation. King George took our money, but we had no voice in parliament.

Rivera   And when did that happen?

S. Adams   1773. Three years after the massacre. Let me tell you, the flame of revolution was beginning to burn bright.

Ryan   And burn it did! The next big event was just about two years later in 1775. And we can see where it all started, right here on the Freedom Trail at the Old North Church.

Rivera   And we've asked Paul Revere to tell us about that. Paul, are you there?

Revere   I am, J D. We knew the British wanted to put that revolutionary flame out, and we knew they were planning to march to Concord to disarm the militia, and we knew they were hot on the trail of Sam Adams and John Hancock, two men who were fanning the flames of liberty.

Rivera   Paul, there's a caller from Seattle who has a question for you.

Seattle   Mr. Revere, I learned about you from Longfellow's famous poem, *Paul Revere's Ride.* I believe a friend put a lantern in the steeple of the Old North Church as a signal that the British were on the way. On April 19th you rode from Boston to Concord to warn the militia.

Revere   That's right. When I saw the signal, I began my ride, along with two friends, William Dawes and Samuel Prescott. We warned people all along the way.

Seattle   Did you get to Concord?

Revere   I only got to Lexington, but Prescott made it all the way and by morning the militia was ready and waiting for the Redcoats. Hancock and Adams got away, but the militia stood their ground and shots were fired.

The Boston Freedom Trail

Seattle   The shot heard 'round the world.

Rivera   Right! And thanks to you and your friends, Paul, the revolution was underway.

Ryan   And just two months later, the colonial army met the Redcoats in the first major battle of the Revolution, the Battle of Bunker Hill.

Rivera   And what happened there, Chris?

Ryan   Well, there were some hills in Charleston, just across the river from Boston. The British planned to fortify the hills, but the colonials got there first and set up defensive positions on one of the hills. The British made three attacks, and on the final attack the colonials retreated.

S. Adams   I'm back again, J D and Chris. Yes, our army retreated, but it was a victorious retreat for our new colonial army. We showed the British that we could and would fight. They attacked with over 2,000 men and by the end of the day, half of them were casualties — 228, dead and 826 wounded. We lost some brave men, too — Over 400 killed or wounded.

Ryan   And that was the real beginning of a bloody war that finally ended six years later.

Rivera   Although that concludes our visit to Boston and the American Revolution, there is still a revolution in Boston, but it's a soccer team, and the patriots are still fighting, but now as a football team. From here, we go on to another revolution, the industrial revolution that got its American start in the city of Lowell, just a few miles north of Boston. Before we go, however, let's open the lines to questions and comments from our listeners.

Lowell
National Historical Park

The Industrial Revolution in America

The falls on the Merrimack

The Industrial Revolution in America began in Lowell, Massachusetts. It is located on the Merrimack River. The river was a source of power for the mills. The principal product was textiles. Many people came to see the Industrial Revolution at the mills in Lowell. In the early years, many of the workers were young women, called "Mill Girls." Then many immigrants came to Lowell. Most of the mills have closed, but Lowell is still a city of many ethnic neighborhoods.

Jean

Time Travelers

J D Rivera, Talk Show Host
Jean Agganis, Park Guide
Francis Cabot Lowell
Sarah Bagley, Mill Girl
Henry David Thoreau, Writer
Jack Kerouac, Writer
Caller from Manchester,
      New Hampshire

Lowell National Historical Park

Jack Kerouac

Henry Thoreau

Rivera   Good morning. This is J D Rivera, your host for *All Around America.* Last week we were in Boston, the birthplace of the American Revolution, and today we are in a city just north of Boston that was the birthplace of the American Industrial Revolution. Welcome to Lowell and the Lowell National Historical Park. I am at the visitor center with Jean Agannis, our guide for today. Jean, why is this place significant?

Agganis   In the early part of the nineteenth century, Lowell became the leader and the model for the American Industrial Revolution. Today, the National Park Service has restored many of the old buildings and mills and turned them into a historical park.

Rivera   So Jean, why here?

Agganis   Basically, there are two main reasons and one of them is the Merrimack River.

Rivera   A river? Interesting. Why was the Merrimack River important?

Agganis   First, the Merrimack is a large river with a significant flow of water, and here in Lowell, the river flows rapidly at Pawtucket Falls.

Rivera   So there was a lot of water power available.

Agganis   Exactly. The force of falling water was used to turn water wheels and turbines which provided the power for the machinery in the mills.

Rivera   And what kind of mills were established here?

Agganis   Textiles. By 1846, the textile mills of Lowell were putting out almost a million yards of cloth every week.

Rivera   You mentioned another reason. What was it?

Lowell   I think that I was the other reason.

Rivera   Is that you, Mr. Lowell? Welcome, and tell us about your city.

Lowell   Actually, J D, I don't know much about the city, but I became quite interested in the industrialization that was happening in England, and so I went there in 1810 to look and learn. I visited several places, but I was especially impressed with Manchester, the center of textile production. In 1814, I returned and with a friend built a successful water-powered mill just outside of Boston.

Rivera   But not in Lowell?

Lowell   Right. I died in 1817, but my associates realized that the Merrimack could provide a great deal of power, and so they began building mills there and named the area Lowell, after me.

Rivera   I see. Well, thanks so much for your call, Mr. Lowell.

Agganis   I can pick up the story from here. By 1830 Lowell was the showplace of American industry. Many famous people came to Lowell to see how this great experiment was changing the ways Americans lived and worked. One of the visitors was the writer Henry David Thoreau.

Rivera   And I think we have Mr. Thoreau on the phone. Mr. Thoreau, what did you see?

Thoreau   Well, I was on the one hand, impressed. I wrote that Lowell was the "Manchester of America, which sends its cotton cloth around the globe."

Rivera   Excuse me, Mr. Thoreau, but we have a caller from Manchester, New Hampshire, with a question.

Manchester Mr. Thoreau, I have been an admirer of your writing for many years, but I am surprised by your comment. You were, in my mind, America's first environmentalist. Didn't you see what was happening to the environment?

Thoreau Of course, I did. In one of my books, I said that fish were once abundant here, but with the construction of the dams and the factories, the fish could no longer exist in the Merrimack.

Manchester And you were right. Here in New Hampshire, the salmon and other fish simply disappeared.

Thoreau I went on to say that after a few thousand years, the factories would disappear and the river would be clear and clean again.

Agganis You were almost right, Mr. Thoreau. But it didn't take a few thousand years. Toward the end of the nineteenth century, the mills in Lowell were in trouble, and by the middle of the twentieth century most of the mills were shut down, and the city of Lowell was in decline.

Manchester J D, I think I know one of the reasons. Other cities throughout the northeast began to compete with Lowell. Right here in Manchester, for example, huge mills also took advantage of the Merrimack and joined the industrial revolution.

Rivera Thanks for your comment, Manchester. So Lowell couldn't keep up.

Agganis Right. And the city was changing in another way, and Sarah Bagley is with us to explain that.

Sarah   Hello, J D and Jean. I was one of thousands of young and mostly single "mill girls" whose labor made the mill owners rich. We came to Lowell because in those days we had few other opportunities. For example, many of us were New England farm girls, and Lowell offered work and good wages. I came here to help support my family back on the farm. We lived in boardinghouses built by the mills. At first, we were happy to have work, and the boardinghouses were clean and well kept.

Rivera   So weren't you happy to be employed?

Sarah   Yes, but we worked 12 hours a day and we began to feel like slaves so we began protesting.

Rivera   And what did the mill owners do?

Sarah   They began to take advantage of the thousands of immigrants who were pouring into America. The immigrants supplied the cheap labor that America's industries needed.

Rivera   And so?

Sarah   And so the mill girls and the boardinghouses disappeared, and the city of Lowell turned into a city of ethnic neighborhoods.

Agganis   I can attest to that. I am descended from a Greek family myself. And even today, Lowell is a city with great ethnic diversity. First, it was the Irish; then the French Canadians, followed by the Greeks, Portuguese, Poles, and in recent years, Cambodians and Hispanics.

Rivera   And on the line with us is a descendant of an immigrant family, Jack Kerouac, another important American writer. Welcome to the show, Mr. Kerouac. Can you tell us a little about your experience growing up in Lowell ?

Lowell National Historical Park

Kerouac   Well, I was born in Lowell in 1922. My parents were French Canadians. At that time in Lowell, almost one-third of all the 100,000 residents were French Canadians. I grew up speaking French and only started to learn English when I went to school.

Rivera   I imagine it wasn't easy growing up.

Kerouac   It wasn't. And it wasn't easy for my family either. The mills were closing, moving to the south, and my father got laid off. I got a scholarship at Columbia University and we moved to New York.

Rivera   And was that when you began your career as a writer?

Kerouac   Yes, it was. Although I dropped out of Columbia, I worked hard at writing. It was discouraging until finally in 1957 my novel *On the Road* became a success.

Rivera   So, your hard work paid off. Thanks for being with us, Jack.

Agganis   And now, J D, there is a festival every year in Jack's honor.

Rivera   And so it's time to wrap up our visit to Lowell and the National Historical Park. This is a story of industrialization, environmental problems, immigration, economic decline, rebirth, and for many immigrants a new life, difficult, but eventually, a success story for many. Our next stop will be a trip back to the difficult years of the American Civil War when we visit the battlefield in Gettysburg, Pennsylvania. But before we go, let's take some comments and questions from our listeners.

Gettysburg
Civil War Battlefield

Gettysburg is a Civil War battlefield in Pennsylvania. The American Civil War was a war between the northern and southern states. The South wanted to be an independent country. At first, the South won many battles, but at Gettysburg, the North won a very big battle. Abraham Lincoln was the president of the northern states. He came to Gettysburg after the battle and gave a very famous speech.

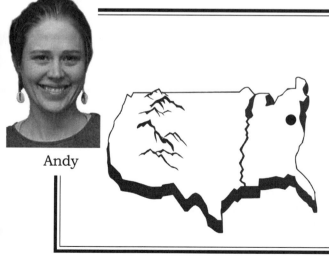

Andy

Time Travelers

J D Rivera, Talk Show Host
Andy Stefanic, Guide at Gettysburg
Abraham Lincoln,
    President of the United States
General Robert E. Lee,
    Commander, Confederate Army
Josephine Smith,
    Citizen from Philadelphia
Caller from Richmond, Virginia
Caller from Montpelier, Vermont

Gettysburg

General Lee   President Lincoln

Rivera Hello everyone and welcome to *All Around America.* Here we are in the beautiful hills of Pennsylvania, at one of the most famous historical places in America, Gettysburg National Military Park. This is your host, J D Rivera, welcoming you to the show which today is focusing on the Civil War, one of the most important and tragic events in American history. So, all you Civil War buffs, get ready with your questions and comments. Andy Stefanic, our guide, is here to take your questions. Welcome to the show, Andy.

Stefanic Thanks, J D, and you're right. The Civil War was one of the most important, if not the most important event in American history. It divided the nation as never before, pitting the North against the South, brother against brother. And this very spot, Gettysburg, is where one of the bloodiest battles of the war took place for three days in July, 1863. It was also the turning point of the war.

Rivera   Tell us a little more about this tragic conflict. What was it all about? Why did America go to war with itself?

Stefanic   Well, in a nutshell, the South wanted to secede from the Union and become an independent country.

Rivera   Why did they want to do that?

Stefanic   The causes were many — economic, social, political, cultural, but certainly the moral question of slavery was a big issue. Slaves were important to the South's economy, and the North opposed slavery. In the end, the South broke away to form its own country. The North, led by President Lincoln, opposed the secession. The tragic result was war.

Rivera   Folks, we are privileged to have with us today one of America's greatest presidents, Abraham Lincoln. Mr. Lincoln, welcome to our show. It's an honor to have you.

Lincoln   Thank you, J D. It's a pleasure to be here.

Rivera   Mr. Lincoln, you were president during the Civil War, weren't you?

Lincoln   Yes, I was, and I can tell you those were terrible, terrible years. After the South seceded, I did not know whether the nation could be saved.

Rivera   Excuse me, Mr. Lincoln, we have a caller from Richmond, Virginia who has a question. Go ahead, Richmond.

Richmond   Mr. Lincoln, why did that war go on for so many years — five, I think. Wasn't the North and its army bigger and stronger? Why didn't the Union Army defeat the Confederate Army right away?

Gettysburg

Lincoln At the beginning of the war, our generals were weak and overly cautious. We had loss after loss, defeat after defeat. But your fellow Virginian, General Robert E. Lee, on the other hand, was a strong, smart leader. In the beginning of the war, he won victory after victory, even though he had a much smaller army. Gettysburg, however, was the first significant victory for the North. It turned the tide.

Richmond I am such an admirer of General Lee. Is it possible, J D, to have him on your show?

Rivera As a matter of fact, he is here with us today. General Lee, what an honor to have you here today!

Lee Thank you, J D. Gettysburg was a tragedy. So many soldiers, many of them just boys, were lost on both sides in just three days. The North lost about 18,000, and we lost more than 20,000. At first, we thought we could win that battle. Our men were ready to fight, but we were outnumbered, and the Northern Army was dug in on top of a hill waiting for us. It was the bloodiest battle of the war.

Rivera General Lee, excuse me, but we have an email from Phoenix, Arizona that asks if the defeat at Gettysburg really broke the back of the South. After Gettysburg, it was just a matter of time, wasn't it?

Lee That's exactly right. Up until then, our Confederate Army was very successful, but after Gettysburg we lost battle after battle. We just couldn't hold off the Union Army.

Rivera Such a tragic part of our nation's history. Let's take our next call from Montpelier, Vermont. You're on the air, Montpelier.

Montpelier   Hello, J D. I'm one of those Civil War buffs you mentioned earlier in the show. I've taken part in many re-enactments of Civil War battles. I have a complete Yankee uniform and an authentic rifle, but I've never been to Gettysburg. I know it's a famous battlefield, but when was it made into a national cemetery?

Stefanic   I can answer that. Congress dedicated the cemetery on November 19, 1863, 16 months before the war was actually over.

Montpelier   If I'm right, Mr. Lincoln, that is when you gave the famous Gettysburg Address, isn't it?

Lincoln   Yes, I was asked to speak at the dedication of Gettysburg, although I was not the main speaker. I had given a lot of thought to what I was going to say.

Montpelier   I heard that you wrote the speech on the back of an envelope. Is that true?

Lincoln   No, I did not write it on the back of an envelope; the occasion was too important. I wanted to honor all the young men who had died. And I wanted to remind the people that the founders of our country created one nation, not two, and it should not perish from the earth.

Rivera   And what a speech that was! In fact, we have someone on the line who was there to hear that speech. Go ahead, Philadelphia.

Smith   This is Josephine Smith. I was with my husband who was a reporter for a Philadelphia paper. He was there covering the dedication. It was a hot day, and Mr. Lincoln was the last speaker. People were already leaving to go home. However, Mr. Lincoln gave a short and powerful speech. It was a speech that will live forever.

Gettysburg

Lincoln   Thank you, madam. My main message was that our young men had not died in vain. However, at the time, I thought my speech did not succeed.

Smith   Well, I was there, and my husband and I both agreed it was one of the greatest speeches ever given. Leaders world-wide began to quote it: "government of the people, by the people, for the people, shall not perish from the earth." In my opinion every school child should memorize it.

Stefanic   I'll go along with that. I can still recite it, and it never gets old. J D, let's take a walk across the battlefield and take a look at the various monuments. Here's one right here from the state of Maine. These memorials are proud reminders of each state that fought at Gettysburg.

Rivera   They are impressive, but this will take us quite a while, so before we walk across this great battlefield, we have to say goodbye to our guests and our listeners. Thank you, callers. Thank you, President Lincoln, and you, General Lee. Please join us again next week when we travel to the great city of Chicago. Before we sign off, we have just time enough for a few more calls.

Chicago
Birthplace of the Skyscraper

The Chicago Fire:
"The Rush for Life Over the Randolph Street Bridge, 1871"
(Harper's Weekly, from a sketch by John R. Chapin)

Chicago is a city of beautiful skyscrapers. It is located on the shore of one of the five Great Lakes, Lake Michigan. It is in the state of Illinois. In 1871 an enormous fire destroyed the city. Famous architects helped rebuild the city. One of them built the world's first skyscraper.

Jackie

Time Travelers

J D Rivera, Talk Show Host
Jackie Williams, Guide
Mike McCormack, Fireman
William LeBaron Jenney, Architect
Louis Sullivan, Architect
Frank Lloyd Wright, Architect
Caller from Birmingham, Alabama

Chicago

W LeB Jenney

L Sullivan

F L Wright

Rivera   Good morning, everyone, and welcome once again to *All Around America,* the show that explores interesting places in our country. This is your host, J D Rivera, welcoming you to one of America's great cities, Chicago, Illinois. You can feel its energy from its busy sidewalks to the top of its magnificent skyscrapers. With me is our guide, Jackie Williams. Welcome to the show, Jackie.

Williams   Glad to be here, J D, and ready to take on the town. Where shall we start?

Rivera   How about kicking our visit off with a little history, Jackie?

Williams   Sure, enough. Most of what you see now can be attributed to the famous Chicago fire of 1871.

Rivera   What do you mean?

Williams   Well, in a nutshell, there was an enormous fire that completely destroyed the city. That was on October 8, 1871. After that, the city had a huge building boom. Chicago basically arose from the ashes, like a phoenix. The beautiful skyscrapers and gorgeous architecture that you see today are the result.

Rivera   Quite a story! I'm sure our listeners have lots of questions. So let's take the first call. From Birmingham, Alabama, you're on the air.

All Around America

Birmingham   Thanks for taking my call. I'd like to know how the fire started.

Williams   The story is that Mrs. O'Leary was milking her cow in the barn, and that the cow kicked over the lantern which started the fire. No one will ever know if this is exactly what happened, but that's what people believed. Mrs. O'Leary claimed that she never had a lantern in the barn, but the story dies hard.

Rivera   Let's talk to one of the firemen who was actually there. Mike McCormack, are you on the line? Can you add anything else?

McCormack   Yes, I'm glad to be here. Let me just say that the fire was a monster, the worst thing I had every seen. For twenty four hours it raged, fanned by a strong wind that had kicked up. We were called to Mrs. O'Leary's place, but somehow in the confusion, we went to the wrong address. By the time we got to her home, the fire was a raging inferno.

Birmingham   So what was the extent of the damage?

McCormack   It killed 300 people and made 100,000 homeless. The cost was 200 million dollars in property destroyed. It was an absolute nightmare. The city was in ruins.

Rivera   What a tragedy!.

Birmingham   So what happened after that? Is that when Chicago began building skyscrapers?

Rivera   I believe so, but let's ask our special guests. We have with us some of the world's best architects. They came to Chicago right after the fire. Let's welcome William LeBaron Jenney, Louis Sullivan, and Frank Lloyd Wright. Gentlemen, great to have you. Now, who would like to field the first question?

27

Chicago

Jenney I'll take it.

Rivera Mr. Jenney, go right ahead.

Jenney The caller is right. After the fire, we architects just flocked to the city. We loved the challenge of rebuilding it. It was an exciting time to be here. We even started a new school of architecture known as the Chicago School.

Birmingham Mr. Jenney, you built the world's first skyscraper, didn't you?

Jenney As a matter of fact, I did. It was the first building to use an all-metal framework. Possibly some of the iron and steel came from your city, Birmingham. The invention of the elevator made it possible to build tall buildings. It was only ten stories high, but for that time, it was significant. It was the Home Insurance Building, built in 1884.

Rivera Thanks, Birmingham, and thanks Mr. Jenney. Jackie, I've been to your great city several times, and love the sky-scrapers here. They are so majestic and graceful. How did the architects achieve that?

Williams Mr. Sullivan, want to take this one? You were very in-volved in creating Chicago's skyscrapers.

Sullivan Yes, I was. I wanted my buildings to express the human spirit. And with the development of iron girders to sup-port each floor, we were able to be much more creative in the designs of our skyscrapers than we were in the past.

Rivera That was quite radical at the time, wasn't it?

Sullivan Yes it was. Also, none of us really wanted to copy the European styles of palaces and Greek temples. We all wanted to create something new.

Rivera   Very interesting! And moving on, we have an email from Kansas City, Missouri, who wants to hear from Mr. Frank Lloyd Wright. She says: "Mr. Wright, your buildings are so unusual. Can you tell a little about your thoughts in designing a building?"

Wright   Basically, it's very simple. I believe that the landscape should be more beautiful after the building was built than before.

Williams   I've seen many of Mr. Wright's buildings. They are always in harmony with the environment, like building into the side of a hill, around a tree, or over a stream.

Wright   That's right. I feel it's essential to work with the natural landscape. You might also want to visit the Unity Church and the homes I designed in Oak Park, not far from here.

Rivera   Thank you, Mr. Wright. Now, Jackie, what do you say we go to the top of the Sears Tower? Is it still the world's tallest building?

Williams   Well, not anymore. It was in 1974 when it was built, but now they're building them higher and higher. Nevertheless, at 110 stories, it's still pretty tall. You can get a great view from the top. But don't get too close to the windows if you have vertigo!

Rivera   Hm. Well, on second thought, Jackie, maybe we'll just stand here on the sidewalk and look up. But let's get out of the wind before we blow away, and changing the subject a little, why is Chicago so windy?

Williams   As a matter of fact, Chicago is called the Windy City. It sits on the shore of Lake Michigan and the winds off the lake are funneled between our tall buildings. Walking our sidewalks can be an adventure. But we Chicagoans call it the Windy City because of all the hot air from our politicians.

Chicago

Rivera It's the same all over, isn't it? But, now unfortunately, it's time to leave this great city. So long, Jackie. Thanks for helping out with our show. For our next stop, we'll head south on Interstate 55 to a city on the great Mississippi River, St. Louis, Missouri. See you there, but we have a few minutes left to take a few more calls from our listeners.

Leiter Building
Sears, Roebuck & Co.
*(the city's oldest
department store)*
*William LeBaron
Jenney,* CHICAGO

Carson Pirie Scott
Department Store
Louis Sullivan, CHICAGO

Robie House, *Classic example of the* Prairie Style
Frank Lloyd Wright, CHICAGO

Sears Tower
Skidmore, Owings and Merrill, LLP
CHICAGO

St. Louis
Gateway to the West

The Gateway Arch

St. Louis is a city on the Mississippi River. It is in the state of Missouri. It is known as the "Gateway to the West." Explorers and pioneers passed through St. Louis on their way to the West. Today a beautiful arch symbolizes the gateway.

Marty

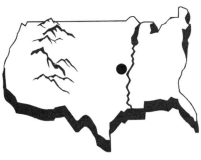

Time Travelers

J D Rivera, Talk Show Host
Marty Marelli, Guide
Meriwether Lewis, Explorer
William Clark, Explorer
Eero Saarinen,
    Architect of the Gateway Arch
Caller from Santa Fe, New Mexico
Caller from Tulsa, Oklahoma

Alaska

William Clark   **Meriwether Lewis**

Rivera This is J D Rivera, welcoming you to another interesting stop on our journey *All Around America.* Today, we are in St. Louis, Missouri, the city known as the Gateway to the West, and with me is our guide, Marty Marelli. Marty, why is St. Louis important?

Martelli Well, historically it was the gateway to the West. In fact, this is where the explorers, Lewis and Clark, began and ended their famous expedition to the Pacific. After that, St. Louis became the starting place for pioneers traveling westward to settle this country.

Rivera Marty, I think this might be a good time to introduce a couple of those travelers. We are delighted to have with us Meriwether Lewis and William Clark, from that famous expedition. Gentlemen, it's good to have you here. I know our listeners would like to know about that historic trip. Would you take some calls?

Lewis We'd be glad to, and let me add that it's a pleasure to be here.

Clark That goes for me, too. My pleasure, also.

Lewis And we have a call from Santa Fe, New Mexico. Do you have a question?

All Around America

Santa Fe Mr. Lewis, I've heard a lot about this expedition, but why did you guys do it? Were you after gold, or something?

Lewis No, it wasn't for gold. In 1803, President Jefferson bought what is known as the Louisiana Purchase from France. It was a huge part of the continent. It stretched from New Orleans to Montana. It included all or part of thirteen states. He wanted to find out more about this land, — its geography, the plants and animals, and the Native Americans who lived here. He wanted to know especially if there was a waterway to the Pacific Ocean. So, the President asked me to head up the expedition, and I got in touch with an old friend, William Clark, to be my co-captain.

Santa Fe But why did you take it on? It was a really risky journey. I understand the territory was unknown and dangerous at that time.

Lewis It surely was. But both Captain Clark and I were deeply interested in exploration. We were frontiersmen, and we loved adventure, and after all, we too, were very curious about what lay west of the Mississippi. Care to add anything, Captain?

Clark As Captain Lewis said, we both love adventure. And we knew it was an opportunity to do something no one had ever done before — be the first to carefully explore the American West. We jumped at the chance. It was the chance of a lifetime. It was too good to pass up.

Santa Fe So, when did your expedition get underway?

Lewis We left St. Louis on May 14, 1804. Our crew of thirty men couldn't wait to get going. The Corps of Discovery — that's what we were called. It was a great day. The citizens of St. Louis cheered as we took off.

Rivera What was it like traveling in the wilderness in those days?

St. Louis

Lewis It was a long and treacherous journey, harder than we had expected. And we met bears, lots of them, especially grizzlies. One of them even chased our men right into their canoe and attacked. It took nine bullets to bring it down. Captain Clark, would you like to add anything?

Clark Sure. We met Indians, some hostile — ready to do us in – – and some friendly and helpful. I can't say enough about the young Indian woman, Sacagawea, who joined the expedition. She helped us tremendously as an interpreter and guide. She even brought her little baby along, carrying him on her back all the way.

Rivera Amazing! And we have a call from Tulsa, Oklahoma. Go ahead, Tulsa.

Tulsa So, when did you two finally reach the Pacific?

Lewis More than a year later, on November 7, 1805, and I can tell you we were overjoyed. But spending the winter there was another matter. It was absolutely depressing. It rained for weeks on end. We sure were glad to get back to St. Louis a year later. That was on Sept 23, 1806.

Tulsa I'll bet they were glad to see you.

Clark Indeed! Until we returned, no one knew whether we were dead or alive. The whole city came out to greet us. They yelled and cheered, and shot their guns into the air. We had a huge party that night.

Rivera What a great welcome! And after that, it seems that others realized it could be done and wanted to go west.

Lewis Yes. They'd heard about the great farm land and they wanted to settle in the wide open spaces.

Rivera Captains Lewis and Clark, thanks so much for being on our show. Did you have another question, Tulsa?

Tulsa This question is for Marty Marelli. I've been to St. Louis, and I was really impressed by the Jefferson National Expansion Memorial with its wonderful Gateway Arch. As a matter of fact, I took a ride right to the top. Can you tell me a little about how it all came about?

Martelli Sure. But first, let me say that the Gateway Arch stands on almost the exact spot from which Lewis and Clark launched their expedition. Now about the Park itself. In 1933, a group of influential citizens got together to create the Jefferson National Expansion Memorial. They wanted to honor Thomas Jefferson, the Louisiana Purchase, and the pioneers who settled the West.

Rivera Marty, here's an email from Newark, New Jersey. It says, "I've only seen the Gateway Arch in pictures. It's so simple and elegant, and somewhat unusual. What did the architect have in mind?"

Martelli No problem in answering that one. We have with us Eero Saarinen, architect of the Arch.

Rivera Mr. Saarinen, would you care to answer that question?

Saarinen Be glad to, and thank you for asking me to the show. First of all, I just want to say that I am an immigrant myself, from Finland, and I was so happy to give something back to this country and create something that symbolizes the westward movement.

Rivera But why an arch?

Saarinen Why not? An arch is a door, and St. Louis was the door for those who passed through here and dared to go west for a new life. Now about the arch. I chose what is called the inverted catenary arch, an upside down chain held on two ends. I have always liked the Roman triumphal arch, so that was my inspiration. My arch would be a gateway to a new life.

St. Louis

Rivera   Most interesting!

Martelli   I love the Arch. When the Mississippi flooded in the summer of 1993, we took inspiration and courage from it. It stayed open all during that awful time. It never closed even though part of its stairway was under water, just as many of our homes were. Mr. Saarinen, we here in St. Louis are very proud of your great achievement.

Saarinen   Thank you. And thank you for inviting me today. It's a real pleasure to know that *All Around America* has stopped at the arch in St. Louis.

Rivera   Well, folks, that brings our show to an end. We have to conclude this most interesting visit to a great little city. Thank you, guests. Thank you, callers. And goodbye until next week when we'll follow in the footsteps of Lewis and Clark up the Missouri River to South Dakota. But there's still time for a few more calls.

**Statue of Lemhi-Shoshone guide Sacagawea
at her birthplace in Idaho**

Mount Rushmore
A Tribute to Four Presidents

Mount Rushmore is a huge sculpture in the Black Hills of South Dakota. The heads of four presidents are carved into the side of a mountain. It was begun in 1927. The sculptor, Gutzon Borglum, died before it was finished. His son finished the sculpture in 1941.

Erin

Time Travelers:

J D Rivera, Talk Show Host
Erin Carlson, Guide
Gutzon Borglum,
    Sculptor of Mount Rushmore
Rafael Sebastiani,
    Worker on the project
Lincoln Borglum, Son of Gutzon
Caller from Raleigh, North Carolina
Caller from Dover, Delaware

Mount Rushmore

Gutzon Borglum

Rivera   Good morning, folks, and welcome to *All Around America,* the timeless talk show that lets you explore some of the great places of our country. Today, we are at another incredible location, Mount Rushmore in the Black Hills of South Dakota. With us, we have Erin Carlson, our guide. Welcome to the show, Erin.

Carlson   Glad to be here.

Rivera   And we also have with us a special guest, Gutzon Borglum, sculptor of Mount Rushmore. Welcome to the show, Mr. Borglum. Are the two of you ready to answer some questions from our listening audience?

Carlson   Yes, I'd be glad to. I really enjoy telling people about Mount Rushmore and the remarkable sculptures carved right into the mountain. Mr. Borglum, they are awesome and inspiring.

Borglum   Thanks, Erin. I really appreciate your enthusiasm because that's exactly what I had in mind when I began the project. I wanted to create something that would remind people of America's greatness.

All Around America

Rivera   I can hardly wait to learn more about Mount Rushmore. The phones are ringing off the hook, and we're ready to take the first call. From Raleigh, North Carolina, you're on the air.

Raleigh   I really enjoy your show, J D. What is Mount Rushmore, anyway? What kind of sculptures are carved into the mountain?

Borglum   Mount Rushmore is a mountain in the southwest region of South Dakota, near Rapid City. The heads of four U.S. presidents: George Washington, Thomas Jefferson, Theodore Roosevelt, and Abraham Lincoln are carved into this mountain.

Raleigh   Can you tell us why you chose these four presidents?

Borglum   Yes, be glad to. I felt that these four presidents would remind people of America's greatness — its birth, represented by Washington; its growth, Jefferson; its preservation, Lincoln; and its development, Roosevelt. For me, these presidents expressed America's vision.

Raleigh   How big are the figures in Mount Rushmore?

Borglum   Each president's face is 60 feet tall. That's as tall as a three-story building. And each is 20 feet wide. I wanted to make the presidents look powerful, just like our country, but noble-looking, too.

Raleigh   So, could you tell us a little about how you actually made these sculptures?

Borglum   Well, of course. We used models to work from. One inch equaled one foot on the actual carving. We didn't have any fancy equipment like you do now. The mountain is granite — hard, white rock — so we had to use dynamite. It was dangerous work — touch and go.

Mount Rushmore

Rivera Thanks for your call, Raleigh, and now a call from Dover, in the state of Delaware, America's first state.

Dover Hi, J D. May I talk to one of the stonecutters who worked on Mount Rushmore?

Rivera Erin, I believe you invited a worker to be here.

Carlson I did. Let me introduce Rafael Sebastiani.

Sebastiani I was one of the workers. Does somebody have a question?

Dover Yes, I do. Mr. Borglum said that the project was important to the nation as a reminder of America's greatness. Did you feel the same way when you worked on it?

Sebastiani Not at first. You see, this was 1927 and the whole country was out of work. It was the Depression, so we were glad to have a job – any job. But as time went by, we got caught up in the whole thing. As we began to see the faces of the four presidents, we knew we were creating something special, a national treasure.

Dover What exactly did you do, Mr. Sebastian.

Sebastiani I did Lincoln's beard and Roosevelt's hair, among other things. Even today, when I look at those sculptures, I feel a special pride.

Rivera I'm sure you do, Rafael. I really get a kick out of talking to people like you who were actually there. Thanks for being with us. Now we have an email from Columbia, South Carolina that asks if anybody got hurt or got killed working with all that dynamite, so high up and in all kinds of weather.

Carlson Fortunately, not a one. We were very lucky.

Rivera   Mr. Borglum, you must have been very proud when it was finally completed.

Lincoln Borglum   Dad, let me answer that. This is Lincoln, Mr. Borglum's son. It took fourteen years to complete. I am sorry to say my father passed away in 1941, so it was my responsibility to finish the work my father had started. Seven months later it was completed.

Rivera   I have read that as monuments go, only the Great Pyramid of Egypt is larger than Mount Rushmore. Is that so?

Lincoln   Almost right. The Great Pyramid of Egypt is larger, but Mount Rushmore stands taller. At any rate, both are beautiful, colossal works of art.

Rivera   So, Erin, anything else you'd like to add before we leave?

Carlson   Gosh, J D, there's so much to see in this corner of South Dakota.

Rivera   So tell me about it.

Carlson   Well, there's the incredible Badlands National Park.

Rivera   Badlands?

Carlson   Bad and beautiful. The earth's surface has been eroded revealing one of the world's richest fossil beds — the remains of plants and animals from 30 million years ago. And we have a great underground park.

Rivera   An underground park?

Carlson   Wind Cave National Park is one of the world's longest caves, and above ground the park includes beautiful prairie grasslands, forests, and lots of wildlife.

Mount Rushmore

Rivera A lot to see. Anything else to add, Erin?

Carlson Only that every year over two million people call on our presidents here at Mount Rushmore.

Rivera Well, we hope you, our listeners, also come for a visit — and bring the kids. It's a great way to learn a little American history. There you have it, folks, another wonderful trip to a memorable place. Thanks to our guests and our callers, and to you, Erin, for arranging our visit here. See you next week when we'll be in Oregon. It's time now for a few last-minute questions.

The Oregon Trail
The Way West to Fortunes and Farmlands

On the Oregon Trail to Portland, 1832

The Oregon Trail is about 2000 miles long. It goes from Missouri to Oregon. About 150 years ago many pioneers with their families traveled the trail in wagons. Many of them were going west for the farmland of the Williamette Valley in Oregon.

Nancy

Time Travelers

J D Rivera, Talk Show Host
Nancy Walker, Guide
Robert Stuart,
    Discoverer of South Pass
Narcissa Whitman, Missionary
Caller from Eugene, Oregon
Caller from Portland, Maine

The Oregon Trail

Narcissa Whitman   **Drawing of Walla Walla**   **Robert Stuart**

Rivera   This is J D Rivera with *All Around America,* the timeless talk show. We're in the state of Oregon at the National Historic Oregon Trail Interpretive Center. We're just outside Baker City, on a hill looking down at a section of the old Oregon Trail. We can still see traces of the trail where thousands of wagons passed by. But why? I've asked a local expert to help us understand. Nancy Walker, tell us about yourself.

Walker   Well, I grew up here in Baker, and I became fascinated by what happened on our doorstep over 150 years ago. Now I'm a volunteer worker here at the center, and I just love telling visitors about this historic trail.

Rivera   So, how about a thumbnail sketch of what happened?

Walker   Whew! There's so much to say. How can I boil it down? The trail begins in Independence, Missouri, and ends near Portland where the Williamette River joins the Columbia. It's about 2000 miles long.

Rivera   Excuse me, Nancy, but we already have a caller from the Williamette Valley. Go ahead, Eugene, Oregon.

Eugene   Hello! Hello! I'm absolutely thrilled that you have featured the Oregon Trail on your program. It's an amazing page in the history of this country.

All Around America

Walker   I couldn't agree more with your caller. It is amazing.

Eugene   My ancestors made that trip in 1843. 2000 miles with two children, a wagon, six oxen, and two cows.

Rivera   And we at *All Around America* followed that trail. Let me tell you, it's a long way, even in our comfortable van, and we didn't have two kids in the back seat. So, caller, how long did it take them? Including our side trip to Mount Rushmore, it took us four days.

Eugene   Months! Usually about five. Remember, they could only go as fast as their feet and their oxen could go — maybe two miles an hour on the flat stretches.

Rivera   Thanks for calling. Now, Nancy, tell us a little about the history of this trail. What's it all about?

Walker   It's about furs, farms — and religion.

Rivera   What do you mean?

Walker   At first, nobody was very interested in Oregon Territory. The British controlled it, but American fur traders began to move in. John Jacob Astor's men founded Astoria at the mouth of the Columbia in 1811, and in 1812, one of his men, Robert Stuart, with a small group of men headed east to tell Astor that one of his ships had been lost.

Rivera   So Stuart traveled the trail backwards, so to speak. And I've asked him to speak to us and tell about his adventure. Are you there, Mr. Stuart?

Stuart   I am. Thanks for having me on the show. It's good to know that someone recognizes what I did.

Rivera   And that was ?

The Oregon Trail

Stuart I discovered the famous South Pass. We knew there was a huge barrier awaiting us as we approached the Continental Divide. Huge mountains to cross. But we found a gap in Wyoming Territory, just south of the Wind River Range. We realized that wagons could make it through the gap, and when we got to St. Louis we told everybody.

Walker J D and Robert, let me point out that nobody paid much attention until twenty years later when Captain Benjamin Bonneville crossed the pass with wagons. Eventually he went on to the Columbia River. Then the word started to spread and the wagon trains began to travel the trail.

Stuart And they built and named a dam on the Columbia after him. But nobody named the South Pass after me.

Rivera Well, a belated thanks for what you did, and thanks for being on the show. You helped make history.

Walker And so he did. Four years after that, Dr. Marcus Whitman joined a group of fur traders and headed west. His goal was to bring Christianity to the Indians, but what was really important was he took his wife with him as well as another missionary and his wife, Eliza Spaulding.

Rivera And Narcissa Whitman is here to tell us about it.

Narcissa Thank you for this chance to tell our story. Still to this day, I thank God that we made it all the way to the Columbia.

Walker It wasn't easy, was it?

Narcissa Not at all, but I thought of our trip as our honeymoon, and in fact, by the time we reached the Snake River in Idaho, I was pregnant.

Walker And your wonderful letters back home persuaded others that women and even children could make it. But you didn't go all the way.

46

Narcissa No, we stopped and established a mission on the Walla Walla River to serve the Indians.

Walker And so, that was the beginning of a huge migration, thousands of wagons heading west. But this time, they were headed for the rich land of the Williamette Valley, where, it was said, farmers could prosper, and life would be wonderful. Over 300,000 made the journey, and at least 30,000 died along the way.

Rivera Excuse me, Nancy. We have a caller. Hello, there, Portland. How's the weather there? We'll be there tomorrow to catch a flight.

Portland The weather here's fine, but I'm calling from Portland, Maine, not Portland, Oregon.

Rivera Oh. Well, anyway, welcome to the show. What's on your mind?

Portland I want to know why there were so many deaths.

Walker Accidents and cholera. A few were killed in Indian attacks, but really not that many. Some drowned, and many were killed by loaded guns going off accidentally. However, the dreaded disease cholera was the number one fear.

Portland Why cholera? I thought you got that from drinking contaminated water. Weren't the rivers in the West clear and clean?

Walker The pioneers brought the disease with them from St. Louis, and when it struck, it killed quickly. They just weren't careful at their campsites. As one wagon train left a campsite, it left behind garbage, dead bodies, and water infected with cholera bacteria, and the next wagon train camped in the middle of all this filth.

Rivera We have time for one more question, Portland.

The Oregon Trail

Portland I know this is a big question, but what can you tell us about how this affected the native populations along the way, the American Indians who called the West their home?

Walker Essentially, it is a sad story. At first the Indians were fascinated with the things the pioneers brought with them, and they wanted these western things: medicine, pots, pans, firearms, and the magic that these white people must possess. But two cultures were on a collision course, and it ended very badly for the Indians. Probably the most sensational event in this sad story occured at the Whitman mission in Walla Walla.

Portland What happened?

Walker The pioneers also brought diseases, and in 1847 at the Whitman mission many Cayuse Indians, with no immunity to measles, caught the disease and died. The Indians may have thought Dr. Whitman was poisoning them. Anyway, they killed the Doctor and Narcissa and several others and burned the mission. When word reached Washington, the government decided to declare Oregon part of the United States to protect the settlers. In short, the culture of the settlers prevailed.

Rivera Our time is up, but here at the Interpretive Center, the story of this incredible migration is kept alive. From here, we will follow the Columbia to the airport in Portland, Oregon, and take off for a visit to the incredible state of Alaska. Thank you, Nancy, for being our guide and historical interpreter. Before we leave, we have time for a few questions from our listeners.

Alaska
Big and Beautiful

Alaska was once owned by Russia, but it was sold to the United States. Many people thought it was a waste of money. But gold was discovered, and many people went to Alaska. Now it is state with great natural beauty, and many people go to enjoy the mountains, glaciers, parks and animals.

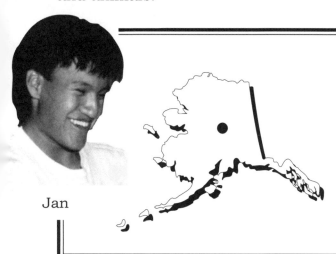

Jan

Time Travelers:

J D Rivera, Talk Show Host
Jan Harris, Alaskan Guide
Vitus Bering, Explorer
William Seward,
    U. S. Secretary of State
Joe McDonald, Gold prospector
Caller from Nashville, Tennessee
Caller from Boise, Idaho

Alaska

*Vitus Bering – a bust
reconstructed from Bering's skull.
Horsens Museum, Denmark*

*William H. Seward
U. S. Secretary of State
1861-1869*

Rivera Good morning, friends, and welcome to our show *All Around America.* You won't believe the incredible place we are broadcasting from today. It's the gorgeous state of Alaska. If you want learn the fascinating history of this state, see the highest mountain and largest glacier in North America, not to mention all kinds of wildlife, this is absolutely the place to be. Right, Jan?

Harris Right you are J D. We have everything here in Alaska and on a grand scale. It is the biggest state. As a matter of fact the name Alaska, or Alyeska, means "great land" in the language of the Aleut people.

Rivera Ladies and gentlemen, I'm talking to our Alaskan guide, Jan Harris. Welcome to the show, Jan. And let's get started right away and take calls from our listening audience. So, go ahead, Nashville.

Nashville Love your show, J D. I'm interested in history, and I understand that at one time Alaska belonged to Russia. How did that happen?

Rivera We have with us Vitus Bering, who can speak to that. Mr. Bering? Can you answer that question?

Bering First, let me say that I am from Denmark, not Russia, but I was employed by the Russians to explore and map the Siberian coast. On my first voyage in 1728 I found the strait that separates Siberia and Alaska, and later in 1741, I discovered the coast of Alaska.

Nashville So, the Russians settled in that area? But, why? Nothing was there, except wilderness.

Bering It was, indeed, a cold and dangerous place. I wrecked my ship on an island and I died there. But I can tell you there was much in Alaska! After my discovery, the Russians discovered seal and otter furs like they had never seen before. They were luxurious and most beautiful. They knew they would bring a good price on the market, so they established a fur trading post. Soon after, Russians began settling there.

Rivera Thank you, Mr. Bering. Since the strait and the sea are named for you, your name lives on.

Harris I'd like to add a few words, if I may. Tragically, those who settled here enslaved my people, the Aleuts. They forced them into hard labor, hunting for fur. Many died. It was a terrible time in Alaska's history.

Rivera Tragic, indeed. You have another question, Nashville?

Nashville So, how come Alaska was sold to the U.S.?

Rivera Mr. Seward, would you like to answer that ? We have with us today William Seward who was the U. S. Secretary of State, and who negotiated the sale at that time. Welcome to the show, Mr. Seward.

Alaska

Seward   Thank you. That was in 1867, and the Russians had approached us on several occasions with an offer to sell. Their country had huge debts from the Crimean War. In addition, the seals had been over-hunted, and the bottom had fallen out of the fur business. They wanted to get rid of Alaska. We bought the land for 7.2 million dollars, at two cents an acre.

Nashville   That was quite a deal!

Seward   Yes, but most Americans didn't think so. They called Alaska "Seward's Icebox" and "Seward's Folly." The newspapers had all kinds of cartoons making fun of the sale. One had me shaking hands with a polar bear. But I knew buying Alaska was good for the country, and then, a few years later, gold was discovered in 1896.

Rivera   Our next caller is from Boise, Idaho. You're on the air.

Boise   That's what I want to talk about — gold. My great grandfather went looking for it in Alaska. May I speak with one of the gold prospectors? Did they actually find gold, or was it just a pipe dream?

Rivera   Joe McDonald, are you there? You were one of the early prospectors, weren't you? Was there any gold?

McDonald   Sure was. We found gold and lots of it, but that's because we were there first. There were many gold strikes, mostly around the Klondike and Yukon Rivers. You can't believe the flood of humanity that came looking for gold. There was a virtual stampede. Why, between 1890 and 1900, the population doubled!

Boise What a life it must have been, everybody rushing to Alaska to strike it rich! What was that like?

McDonald It was sheer misery. Alaska was a wild country — few towns and no roads. You had to be pretty hardy to survive. Why, walking up mountains with everything you owned on your back was almost enough to kill a man. It was no picnic, let me tell you — bad food, miserable weather, dangerous animals, and on top of all that, greedy merchants who tried to take you for every cent you had. It was a rough life, to say the least.

Harris Let me add that today, hikers can take the "Trail of Misery," which is the actual trail that the early prospectors traveled on to get to the gold towns. It's been turned into the Klondike Gold Rush National Historical Park in Skagway.

Rivera Thanks for being on the show, Joe. Now we have an email from Buffalo, New York that asks "Who lives in Alaska today? Mainly Eskimos?"

Harris Oh, no. Roughly 75% are Whites, and only about 15% are Native Alaskans such as Native Indian tribes and Eskimos. The rest are a mixture of people from all over the world. And by the way, many Eskimos prefer to be called "Inuit" which in their language means "The People."

Rivera Quite a history lesson we're getting today! But, Jan, tell us more about Alaska today. Do you get a lot of visitors?

Harris Yes, we do. Next to fishing and oil, tourism is our principal industry. People want to see the glaciers, the mountains, and the wildlife.

Alaska

Rivera   Does Alaska have any national parks?

Harris   You bet ! We have eight. And thousands of visitors want to climb Mount McKinley, North America's highest mountain, in Denali National Park. Others prefer a cruise from which they can look at the stupendous glaciers. And we have the famous Iditarod Dog Sled Race from Anchorage to Nome. Mushers — that's what we call dog sledders — come from all over the world to compete.

Rivera   And you haven't even mentioned the Arctic Circle where in summer it's actually light twenty-four hours a day.

Harris   That's true. At that time, we have all kinds of special native art and dance festivals, writing conferences, even a midnight baseball game to celebrate the twenty-four hours of daylight.

Rivera   What a great place to visit! Folks, you need time, lots of time to visit this great state. Jan tells me there are three million lakes, 1,800 islands and 5,000 glaciers. Sadly, we have to bid goodbye to our 49th state and remind you to join us at another great place when *All Around America* takes to the air again for a flight south to our 50th state, Hawaii — a state that is so different from Alaska. So, listeners, before we leave, what else would you like to know about Alaska?

**Mount Mckinley
or Denali**

Hawaii

The Aloha State

Hawaii is a beautiful island state in the Pacific Ocean. It was settled by Polynesians who established a monarchy under King Kamehameha. Captain James Cook discovered the islands, and then Americans slowly began to take control of the economy and the government. Hawaii became a state in 1959.

Lydia

Time Travelers

J D Rivera, Talk Show Host
Lydia Suzuki, Guide
Kamehameha I,
    Founder of the Kingdom of Hawaii
Reverend Hiram Bingham, Missionary
Queen Liliuokalani
Caller from St. Paul, Minnesota
Caller from Salt Lake City, Utah

Hawaii

King Kamehameha I   **Queen Liliuokalani**

Rivera   Aloha, friends and listeners. This is your host, J D Rivera, along with our guide, Lydia Suzuki, welcoming you to *All Around America.* Today we are in paradise. That's right, I said paradise, for that's what Hawaii is — heavenly islands with lush vegetation, perfumed flowers, wide sandy beaches, huge volcanoes, fantastic waterfalls, the great blue Pacific Ocean, and of course, perfect weather all year long. Lydia, I think I want to live here! Let's trade places.

Suzuki   I don't think I'll take you up on that, J D, but I'm not surprised at your reaction to our state. Hawaii does attract millions of people every year, but lucky for us Hawaiians, they don't all settle down. They're tourists and very important to the economy of our island.

Rivera   So tell me a little about the people who do live here on the islands.

Suzuki   Well, about one-eighth of our population are the native Hawaiians or Polynesians, the original people. The rest are a mixture of Asian and White people. We are the only state that does not have an ethnic majority.

Rivera   Very interesting. So, Lydia, the Polynesians were the first people here.

Suzuki   Yes. They came from the Marquesas Islands, 2000 miles away about 1,500 years ago. The islands were pretty isolated until 1778 when James Cook, the famous English explorer, discovered them. He named them the Sandwich Islands, and came back in 1779. Unfortunately, he was killed in a fight with the native Hawaiians.

Rivera   What happened after the discovery?

Suzuki   Well, that pretty much opened the door for others to come. And before you knew it, whalers, traders, missionaries, and greedy businessmen began pouring in. Everybody wanted a piece of Hawaii.

Rivera   Well, I can see why. Now let's take our first call. St. Paul, Minnesota, go ahead.

St. Paul   Thanks for taking my call. I've been to Hawaii, and I saw a statue of King Kamehameha the First on Oahu, and there are many places named after him. Who was he, and what did he do?

Rivera   You're in luck because we were able to get King Kamehameha to be with us. Your Majesty, can you take this caller's question?

Kamehameha   Aloha. Let me say before I became king, the islands were divided and ruled by local chiefs who were constantly at war. I defeated the chiefs, and in 1795, united the islands and founded the Kingdom of Hawaii.

Suzuki   I want to add that the people loved King Kamehameha the First. He brought peace to the islands.

St. Paul   I think that there were several kings named Kamehameha. Am I right?

Hawaii

Kamehameha	That's correct. I was the first, and my son was the second. Eventually there were five Kamehamehas. The dynasty lasted until 1872 when Kamehameha the Fifth died without leaving an heir to the throne.
St. Paul	And I've heard that missionaries did plenty of damage to Hawaiian culture when they came. They tried to wipe out their customs and traditions, didn't they?
Rivera	Reverend Bingham, do you want to defend yourself? You were among the first missionaries who came to the islands, beginning in the 1820s.
Bingham	That's right, I was. We were shocked by the nakedness of the people and the hula dances they performed. So, we introduced long dresses for the women and banned hula dancing. However, we also built churches and schools and taught the natives how to read and write.
Kamehameha	All this happened after my time, and it began a long series of changes — perhaps for the good, perhaps not.
Bingham	But change was inevitable.
Kamehameha	Probably. But I wonder if the changes improved our lives.
Rivera	Gentlemen, thank you for being on our show. Right now, we have another caller. Salt Lake, are you there?
Salt Lake	Here, dude! I've been to the islands many times. I go for surfing. Man, those twenty-five foot waves are really something. I think Hawaii has got some of the best surfing in the world.
Suzuki	I couldn't agree more. Barely a day goes by that I don't try to get out and catch a wave.

Salt Lake Cool! Next time I come, let's get together. But anyway, I wanted to ask about something serious. I mean the Hawaiian people were robbed by the U.S. Didn't we basically steal Hawaii? What's the scoop on this?

Rivera Let's see if we can find out. We have Queen Liliuokalani who can speak about this. Welcome to the show, Your Majesty.

Liliuokalani Aloha and thank you for inviting me. Yes, I would be happy to answer these questions. When I came to the throne – that was in 1891 – powerful American businessmen had a strong foothold in Hawaii. They were coming in, buying land, taking over, and making a fortune in sugarcane and pineapples, our principal crops.

Rivera So what happened?

Liliuokalani I wanted to make sure that they did not take over completely, so we rewrote the constitution putting more Hawaiians in important jobs in the government. Also, we brought back some of our old customs and traditions. We thought that was important.

Salt Lake Your reign didn't last very long, did it?

Liliuokalani Sadly, no. Two years later, my monarchy was overthrown, and I was imprisoned. These businessmen made Sanford B. Dole president of the Republic of Hawaii, and the monarchy ended. Shortly after, the U.S. annexed Hawaii, and finally, in 1959, it became the fiftieth state.

Suzuki I'd like to add that in 1998, President Clinton signed a formal apology to the Hawaiian people for the overthrow of the monarchy.

Salt Lake Hah! Better late than never, I guess. Thanks for the history lesson. I thought I was right.

Hawaii

Rivera Thanks for your call, Salt Lake. So, Lydia, now that we've covered some of Hawaii's history, we have an email from San Diego, California, that asks, "How many islands are there?" So, tell us a little more about the islands.

Suzuki Well, as you may know, we have eight main islands. We're on Maui, the Garden Island, known for its lush beauty. Oahu is quite metropolitan with theaters, museums, and great restaurants in Honolulu. The U.S.S. Arizona National Memorial at Pearl Harbor is on Oahu, too. But if you really want to see something different, go to the Big Island, Hawaii. It has black sandy beaches and active volcanoes.

Rivera You're kidding! Black beaches? Active volcanoes?

Suzuki Black as coal. And, you can actually see the bubbling lava in the volcanoes. As a matter of fact, all our islands were formed from volcanoes which erupted from under the sea.

Rivera We're running out of time, Lydia, so unfortunately we'll have to come here again. I think we need to explore each island, one at a time.

Suzuki That's the only way to do it, J D.

Rivera For now, we have to say, "Ahui hou aku," goodbye until we meet again. From the Aloha State, this is J D Rivera. Join us again for our next program when we go back to the mainland and the city of San Francisco. But we have a few more minutes for our listeners to call in with their questions and comments.

Queen Liliuokalani's home, Washington Place

The Golden Gate Bridge
San Francisco's Famous Landmark

The Golden Gate Bridge in San Francisco is a wonderful and majestic structure. It crosses the narrow strait between the Pacific Ocean and San Francisco Bay. The bridge is actually orange in color, so it blends with the natural surroundings. It is an architectural triumph.

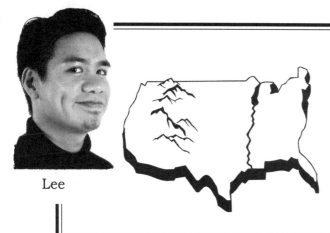

Lee

Time Travelers

J D Rivera, Talk Show Host
Lee Wong, Guide
Joseph B. Strauss, Chief Engineer
Irving F. Morrow,
    Architect and Designer
Caller from Atlanta, Georgia
Caller from Helena, Montana
Caller from Topeka, Kansas

The Golden Gate Bridge

Irving F. Morrow   Joseph B. Strauss

Rivera Good morning, folks, and welcome to *The Time Traveler's Talk Show* that takes you to spectacular places *All Around America.* Well, here we are standing on one of the largest and most beautiful bridges in the world, the Golden Gate Bridge in San Francisco. Before we go on, let me introduce our guide, Lee Wong. Welcome, Lee! Is this an incredible sight or what?

Wong Absolutely spectacular! There's the Bay on our right and the Pacific Ocean on our left. This bridge crosses the entrance to the Bay. And over there is the city of San Francisco, the City by the Bay, as it is called.

Rivera But, Lee, I'm surprised. The bridge is orange. I thought it would be gold in color. How did that come about?

Wong Actually, the architect, Irving F. Morrow, decided that the color orange would blend in better with the natural setting of this beautiful harbor. I understand Mr. Morrow is with us today. Is that right?

Morrow Right here, Lee. Actually the real color is known as International Orange, and I chose it for the reason you suggest. As you can see, it blends in wonderfully with the natural surroundings.

All Around America

Rivera   OK, folks, we've got lots of callers, so let's get to the phones. First caller, from Atlanta, Georgia, what's your question?

Atlanta   Hi, y'all. What I want to know is why is it called the Golden Gate if it's not gold?

Wong   I think I can answer that. It's named after the Golden Strait, the narrow waterway that the bridge crosses. It seems that John C. Fremont, a surveyor in California, came upon it, and as the story goes, it reminded him of the Golden Horn in Istanbul, so he named it the Golden Strait. That was in 1846.

Atlanta   Oh, I get it. So, when the bridge was built, they named it the Golden Gate Bridge after the Golden Strait. Makes sense to me.

Rivera   Thanks, Atlanta, for bringing that up. Now I think we've cleared up the question of the orange Golden Gate. Let's take another call. Helena, Montana, you're on *All Around America.*

Helena   Thanks for taking my call. I've been to San Francisco, and I just want to say that the bridge is incredible. Who built it?

Rivera   You're in luck! We have with us Joseph B. Strauss, chief engineer of the Golden Gate. Mr. Strauss, are you there?

Strauss   Yes, I am. I submitted the original plans for the bridge. Of course, we changed our minds and redesigned the original plans, and we came up with the idea of a suspension bridge. It was a real challenge because of the length of the bridge. It's over a mile long, and the currents underneath are treacherous.

Helena   Can you explain how a suspension bridge works?

The Golden Gate Bridge

Strauss   Well, it's simple in theory. We have two huge towers, 746 feet above water, to be exact, on either side of the bridge. These two towers hold up two steel cables, about 36 inches in diameter. Then there are lots of vertical cables that hold up the roadway. That's it in a nutshell.

Helena   The construction must have been difficult. Was anyone hurt or killed during construction?

Strauss   Believe it or not, nobody was seriously injured or killed. For one thing, we had introduced hard hats for the men to wear. Actually, nineteen workers fell off the bridge, but we had safety nets under the bridge.

Helena   Really? That's amazing. How long did it take to build the bridge?

Wong   Only four years, from 1933 to 1937. It opened ahead of schedule and under budget. That's something that doesn't happen very often.

Rivera   You can say that again, and now we have a call from Topeka, Kansas. What's your question?

Topeka   I've been to San Francisco, and have seen the Golden Gate. It is majestic, beautiful, and inspiring. I can't think up enough adjectives to describe it. I'm studying architecture, and I'd like to know more about the artistic design of the bridge.

Rivera   Mr. Morrow, want to take that question? As the architect, you worked on the design, didn't you?

Morrow   Actually, my wife and I did. First of all, I want to tell you I felt very privileged to be working on it. I knew the bridge was going to be a unique structure, so I did whatever I could to give it a feeling of grandeur and dignity.

Topeka   So, how did you accomplish that?

Morrow   Well, first, I wanted to use the sun's light to accentuate the bridge, so we designed the towers in a special way to catch the sunlight. Also, you'll notice that the portals or openings on the towers are smaller and smaller as they go higher and higher. This gives the effect of the bridge going off into space. It's an incredible illusion.

Topeka   That's true. It does look as if it goes off into space.

Morrow   And, if you come at night, you'll notice the subtle lighting that we designed. It gives the bridge a special glow.

Rivera   We'll, be sure to do that, too. Thanks for being on our show, Mr. Morrow. I can't tell you how inspired I am just being here. I'm going to stick around a while, and take it all in. As a matter of fact, I think I'll join the other pedestrians and joggers crossing the Bridge. What do you say, Lee, shall we jog across?

Wong   Thanks, J D, but I've got to get back to work.

Rivera   Before you go, Lee, tell me about that island I see out in the middle of the bay.

Wong   That's Alcatraz, the infamous prison. It was the island home for many of the nation's worst criminals until it closed in 1973.

The Golden Gate Bridge

Rivera Not really an island paradise like Hawaii, then.

Wong You can say that again. But it is worth an afternoon visit. It's now open to the public and it has a fascinating history. Anyway, before you leave our beautiful city, don't forget to see some of San Francisco's other famous places. We've got lots to offer, like Chinatown, Fisherman's Wharf, and a ride on our famous cable cars. And not far from this spot are the giant redwood trees of Muir Woods.

Rivera Thanks, Lee. Will do. For now, we have to say goodbye. Thank you listeners, callers, and guests for another wonderful stop at one of the most spectacular places all around America, the Golden Gate Bridge. Please join us for our next show when we travel from this man-made wonder to an incredible natural wonder, the Grand Canyon. Now let's give our listeners a few more minutes to call in.

Alcatraz

The Grand Canyon
America's Great Natural Wonder

The Grand Canyon was formed by the Colorado River. It is an enormous canyon. It was first explored by John Wesley Powell in 1869. President Theodore Roosevelt helped to preserve this natural wonder, and today, it is a national park

Kit

Time Travelers

J D Rivera, Talk Show Host
Kit Wilkins, Grand Canyon Guide
John Wesley Powell, Explorer
President Theodore Roosevelt
Caller from Madison, Wisconsin
Caller from Lincoln, Nebraska
Caller from Jackson, Mississippi

The Grand Canyon

John Wesley Powell

Theodore Roosevelt

Rivera Ladies and gentlemen, good morning, and welcome to *All Around America*. Folks, I don't think I can adequately describe the area we are in today. It is just too awesome for words. We are talking about the Grand Canyon, in the state of Arizona, a place like no other on earth, right, Kit?

Wilkins Right! This canyon is enormous — 227 miles long, one mile deep and 18 miles across. Huge doesn't begin to describe it.

Rivera Before, I get too far ahead of myself, let me introduce our guide, Kit Wilkins. Welcome to the show.

Wilkins My pleasure. And, you're right. You just can't put into words the beauty, grandeur, and size of this place.

Rivera I just want to say to our listeners, save your money, and get yourself out here. You will not be disappointed. But for now, let's get to the phones. Madison, Wisconsin, you're on the air.

Madison   Thanks for taking my call. I certainly agree that it's one of the grandest places on earth. I took my family there last summer. I couldn't believe the size, but what really got me were the changing colors of the canyon — red, orange, purple, yellow — different colors at different times of the day. It's quite a show! But what I want to ask is, did any Indians live here at one time or another?

Wilkins   Yes, they did—the Anasazi, the Pueblo, the Hopi, the Paiutes all lived here. And of course, even today, the Havasupai Indians have a small reservation located along the Havasu Creek at the bottom of the Canyon.

Madison   I love sports, and when I was at the Canyon last year, I heard about whitewater rafting on the Colorado River. Can you tell me a little about that?

Wilkins   Now, you're talking. It's my favorite sport. The Colorado offers some of the best in whitewater rafting.   It's really fast and exciting.

Rivera   Speaking of which, let me introduce the very first man who, in 1869, explored the Colorado River and literally put the Grand Canyon on the map. Major John Wesley Powell, welcome to the show, and tell us how you first became interested in the Grand Canyon.

Powell   Thank you and glad to be here. Well, as a professor of geology, I'd always been interested in the natural world. So, after the Civil War where, incidentally, I lost my arm, I wanted to explore a part of our nation that had never been explored or mapped. This area was called the "Unknown." The idea of doing something no one else had ever attempted really caught my imagination, so I got together a crew of nine men, and we set off for the unknown.

Rivera   Next call. Jackson, Mississippi, what's your question?

The Grand Canyon

Jackson   Hello, J D. As you know, our state has a pretty big river, and I'd like to know more about the Colorado. Mr. Powell, I've read about your trip down the Colorado. It was both a triumph and a tragedy, wasn't it?

Powell   Yes, that's quite right. After ninety-eight harrowing days on the river, we finally reached the river's end. We were half-dead with exhaustion. Tragically though, we lost three men.

Jackson   How did that happen?

Powell   Well, as I said, it was a very harrowing trip. Almost nothing went right. The wooden boats were too heavy, the river was much more ferocious than we had ever expected, and the waterfalls were huge. And we were running out of food. It was almost more than we could bear. Everyone's nerves were on edge. So when we came to yet another monster fall, three of our men dropped out of the expedition. They decided to take their chances by trying to find their way out of the canyon rather than possibly drowning in the rapids.

Jackson   And?

Powell   They were never heard from again.

Jackson   What a grim story.

Powell   We barely survived as well. The waterfalls, some as high as Niagara, almost did us in. Since the river had never been charted, we had no idea what awaited us around each bend. It was the most difficult venture of my life.

Wilkins   Your listeners might want to know that Mr. Powell was hailed as "the conqueror of the Colorado," when he returned. It was an incredible feat. Compared to that expedition, today's rafting down the Colorado is a walk in the park with modern boats, maps, and all.

Rivera   And speaking of a walk in the park, tourists can hike the Canyon, can't they, Kit.

Wilkins   Oh yes, and many do. But every year, we have to call up Rescue to bring in a helicopter for someone who's lost or injured. It's a treacherous climb down to the bottom. You're better off riding a mule down.

Rivera   Good suggestion. But let's get back to the Canyon itself. Did early American settlers come to see the Canyon, as people do today?

Wilkins   Oh, yes. Thanks to Mr. Powell, people realized that the Canyon was not inaccessible. But they came for a different reason. Prospectors hoped to strike it rich. They were sure they could find gold there. However, they found no gold. Instead they found other valuable minerals such as copper and asbestos.

Rivera   Let's take our last call from Lincoln, Nebraska, like Madison and Jackson, another city named for a president.

Lincoln   And I'd like to speak with a president, namely President Theodore Roosevelt. Is he there?

Rivera   I believe he is on the line. Mr. Roosevelt?

Roosevelt   Yes, I am delighted to be with you. What's your question, Lincoln?

The Grand Canyon

Lincoln Mr. Roosevelt, I just want to thank you for all your efforts in establishing and preserving national parks while you were president.

Roosevelt Why, thank you. I am proud to be known as the conservation president. I thought it was very important that places like the Grand Canyon be preserved for our children and for our children's children. I insisted that Congress protect our natural resources.

Lincoln So when did Congress actually establish Grand Canyon National Park?

Roosevelt It didn't happen while I was president. However, I fought very hard for it, and I did get it protected as a national monument in 1908. Eleven years later, Congress made it a national park.

Rivera We'd like to add our thanks, too, Mr. President. But for now, we have to say goodbye to the Grand Canyon, our guests, and our listeners. Please join us next week in Colorado where the great river comes from. We'll visit another National Park, Mesa Verde, a national park that was established during Theodore Roosevelt's presidency. There's time now for a few more calls. The lines are open.

Mesa Verde

Home of the Ancient Anasazi

Mesa Verde National Park is in the state of Colorado. Years ago, it was the home of the Anasazi, a native American people. Their cliff dwellings were built into the side of a cliff. In the 1300s, they abandoned the area and moved south to New Mexico and Arizona. Their descendants are the Pueblo people.

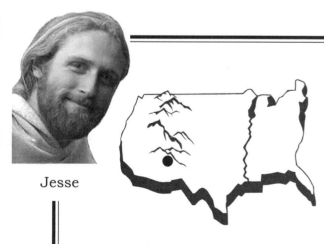

Jesse

Time Travelers

J D Rivera, Talk Show Host
Jesse Jones, Mesa Verde Guide
Running Deer, Anasazi Indian
Swift Arrow, Pueblo Indian
Caller from Indianapolis, Indiana
Caller from Louisville, Kentucky

Mesa Verde

Running Deer

Swift Arrow

Rivera Welcome to *All Around America,* the amazing radio talk show that takes you to famous landmarks in America, and where are we today? I'll let our guide, national park ranger, Jesse Jones, tell us. Jesse, what is this place, anyway? I've never seen anything like it.

Jones Well, we are at Mesa Verde National Park in the beautiful, mountainous state of Colorado.

Rivera Jesse, can you tell our listeners what Mesa Verde means?

Jones In Spanish, "mesa" means table, and "verde" means green. So, it's a green table. In other words, it's a high plateau that has vegetation — grass and trees. And specifically, we are standing in an ancient village that is built on a shelf on the side of a cliff. This was the home of the ancient Indian group called the Anasazi. This one is called the "Cliff Palace."

Rivera Wow! It's hard to believe that people actually lived here, on a shelf in the side of a cliff. How high are we, anyway?

Jones We're pretty high up, about 700 feet off the ground.

All Around America

Rivera   I know our callers have lots of questions, so let's take caller number one from an appropriate city and state, Indianapolis, Indiana. Are you there, Indianapolis? Who do you want to talk to?

Indianapolis   I'd like to talk to a member of the Anasazi tribe, if I may.

Jones   J D, we have a young woman here who can talk to our caller.

Rivera   Great! Who is she?

Running Deer   My name is Running Deer. I am an Anasazi. What would the caller like to ask?

Indianapolis   My question is: Why would anybody want to live on a cliff? It seems so unusual, so dangerous.

Running Deer   My parents never really told me why we built our homes here. We just took it for granted. It just seemed natural for us to live in this place. My guess is that it was for protection. We used ladders to get up and down the cliff. If an enemy approached, we would pull up the ladders. It's pretty hard for the enemy to attack up the side of a cliff.

Indianapolis   How long did you live there?

Running Deer   In these cliff dwellings only about 200 years, but we lived on Mesa Verde — the table top — for a long time. We are a very old culture. Other tribes called us "the ancient ones." Our ancestors lived and worked on top of the Mesa for over a thousand years.

Indianapolis   So where are the Anasazi today?

Mesa Verde

Swift Arrow I think I can answer that. There are no Anasazi living today. I am Swift Arrow, a descendant of the Anasazi. In 1300, something very strange happened. The Anasazi moved away and abandoned Mesa Verde permanently and came south to live in what is now New Mexico and Arizona.

Running Deer That's right. Around that time, we had a terrible drought. It went on 24 years, so I believe we left because we had no choice, we had to — to find food. I was just a little girl when it all happened.

Jones We also think that the soil was depleted, so it became impossible to grow food. All that remains today are these incredible Anasazi structures. Just think! All this happened about 300 years before Europeans began to live in North America.

Rivera That's really interesting! Next question comes from Louisville, Kentucky. Go ahead, Louisville.

Louisville Hello, J D. I wonder if Jesse Jones can you give us an idea of how many people lived on the Mesa at one time. And, by the way, wasn't that a dangerous place for kids? Didn't they fall off the cliff?

Jones As far as we know, at one time 1,000 people lived here. They had a thriving community and even their own government. As a matter of fact, an important part of the Anasazi community was known as the "kiva," a very large council room where we are standing right now.

Running Deer May I add something here?

Rivera Of course, Running Deer, any time.

76

Running Deer My father used to go there with the other men to talk over and decide important community matters. And I remember going there for religious ceremonies. It was a very special place.

Rivera Anyone want to take the question about falling off the cliff?

Swift Arrow I'll take that. Simply put, they were careful. Like all parents, they watched their children closely. And anyway, they spent most of their time on top of the mesa in their fields. They were food growers and gatherers. And the Anasazi parents and children were together most of the day, working the land or in our dwellings making pottery. Right, Running Deer?

Running Deer Absolutely! I spent almost all of my time with my mother, making baskets and pottery and preparing food. She taught me everything. I looked up to her.

Swift Arrow I think most Native American people looked up to their elders. Older people were very valuable members of the community.

Louisville Hm — Things are a little different nowadays. I also wanted to ask if archeologists have dug up many artifacts?

Jones Yes, they have. Mostly, they found beautiful pottery and evidence of beautiful, hand-crafted baskets. In fact, the early Anasazi were known as "the Basket People."

Swift Arrow I just want to say that even today, the descendants of the Anasazi, the Pueblo, carry on these traditions.

Mesa Verde

Rivera   Swift Arrow, we have an email from Philadelphia with a question: "Where do the descendants of the Anasazi live today?"

Swift Arrow   We are the Hopi of Northeastern Arizona, the Zuñi of western New Mexico, and we Taos here in northern New Mexico. I would like to invite you all to my pueblo in Taos, New Mexico, so that you can see for yourself a little of life long ago. We are very proud of our heritage.

Rivera   Well, for me, it's been an awesome experience just walking in the footsteps of an ancient people. Callers, thank you so much for your questions, and guests, thank you for a most interesting journey back in time at Mesa Verde National Park. Swift Arrow, we'll definitely see you at your pueblo in Taos on our way to next week's program in San Antonio, Texas. And now the phones are open for a few more calls.

Remember the Alamo!

Texas' War for Independence

The Alamo is an old mission in San Antonio, Texas. During the Texas War for Independence from Mexico, American fighters were trapped inside the Alamo. After several days of fighting, they were all killed, except a few women, children, and slaves who told what happened. "Remember the Alamo!" became the cry for independence.

Maria

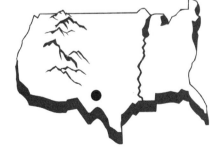

Time Travelers

J D Rivera: Talk Show Host
Maria Hernandez, Guide
Colonel William B. Travis
Davey Crockett, Frontiersman
Santa Anna,
    Mexican General and Dictator
Sam Houston,
    Commander of Texan Army
Caller from Des Moines, Iowa

Remember the Alamo!

| Sam Houston | Davy Crockett | Santa Anna |

Rivera Welcome to *All Around America,* the amazing mobile talk show in which you can talk to famous people across time from historic landmarks all across America. Today, we're broadcasting from inside the Alamo, a famous mission in San Antonio, Texas. With us is our guide, Maria Hernandez. Welcome to the show, Maria.

Hernandez Thanks, J D. Glad to be here.

Rivera First of all, Maria, let's tell our listeners what a mission is.

Hernandez Well, a mission is usually composed of a church and a monastery, enclosed with high walls, often with surrounding farmland. Missions were originally built by the Spanish to spread Christianity in the new world. However, this particular mission was also used as a fort in a battle between Americans and Mexicans.

Rivera Hmm — a fight between America and Mexico? Can you give us a little historical background on that?

Hernandez   Briefly, here's what happened. In 1836, Texas belonged to Mexico. However, there were many more Americans than Mexicans here, and the Americans wanted their independence. They didn't want to live under the Mexican dictator, Santa Anna. Of course, Mexico was not about to give independence to them. They were considered American rebels. So, that's why the fighting began.

Rivera   That's very interesting. Listen, we've got all kinds of important guests with us on the line, the men who actually fought at this battle. We've got Colonel Travis, Davy Crockett, and of course, Santa Anna. We also have Sam Houston, the first governor and president of Texas. Let's take our first caller. From Des Moines, Iowa, you're on the air.

Des Moines   Hello, J D. I'd like to speak with General Santa Anna.

Santa Anna   Bueno! Yes, this is General Santa Anna.

Des Moines   General, you were also a dictator, weren't you?

Santa Anna   Yes, but Mexico needed a dictator at that time. It needed a strong ruler after Spain left Mexico. I felt it was necessary to take control and dissolve the Constitution. It's true, I ruled with an iron hand.

Des Moines   Why did you attack the Alamo?

Santa Anna   Well, you Americans were in Mexican territory. Would you believe that Americans were illegally immigrating into Mexico? We had just gotten Spain out of Mexico, and now we wanted to get the illegal Americans out, too. Then, some American rebels attacked some Mexican villages, so this was revenge. I wanted to show them they couldn't push me around.

Remember the Alamo!

Rivera Well, that's telling it like it was.

Des Moines Now I'd like to ask Colonel Travis a question. You were there. So tell us what happened.

Travis Well, on February 23, 1836, 5,000 of Santa Anna's men approached the mission. We were pretty confident that we could hold them off because we were expecting reinforcements, but they never showed up. We did, in fact, hold out for eleven days, even though we were outnumbered thirty to one. We refused to give up.

Crockett Let me jump in here. I was there with "Old Betsy," my trusted rifle. I'd been a frontiersman in Tennessee, and I'd fought many wild animals, but this was unlike anything I'd ever seen. Thirty to one, imagine that! But, I'll tell you, we fought like tigers.

Travis Davey, you and "Old Betsy" were an inspiration to all of us at the Alamo. We were pinned down, surrounded, and we couldn't escape.

Crockett As the Colonel said, the reinforcements never came, but we held out as long as we could.

Travis We ran out of ammunition, and fought with everything we could. Every single man was killed — all 182 of us.

Rivera So no one got out?

Travis I heard that Santa Anna let some women, children and negro slaves escape. And they were able to tell the story of the battle.

Rivera We have an emailer from Spokane, Washington, who wants to ask Sam Houston how he managed to get a city named after him.

Houston   Well, in a way, I was the George Washington of Texas. I was the commanding general of the Texas army. Our battle cry became "Remember the Alamo!" and we finally captured Santa Anna, sent the Mexicans back to Mexico, and declared independence.

Rivera   So, how exactly did you capture Santa Anna?

Houston   Well, first we beefed up our army, and then a month later went after him. There was no stopping us. We captured him in a surprise attack in San Jacinto, now called Houston. We made him sign a treaty that made Texas an independent nation, and I became the first president.

Rivera   Here's another email. A person from Minneapolis, Minnesota, wants to know if Texas did, in fact, become an independent country.

Houston   That's right. Texas was an independent country for about ten years. In 1845, we became the 28th state. I want to say that I am proud of my role in establishing Texas as part of America.

Rivera   Well, there you have it, folks, a little history from the Alamo in San Antonio, Texas. Maria, I understand there are actually several missions that tourists can visit here in San Antonio.

Hernandez   That's true, J D. You can drive the Mission Trail and see five historic Spanish missions from the eighteenth century, but of course the Alamo is the best known. Today it is owned by the state of Texas, and thousands visit it every year. And there's another trail that is important in San Antonio's history — the Chisholm Trail.

Rivera   What's that about?

Remember the Alamo!

Hernandez   I'm sure you know that cattle ranching has always been very important in Texas.

Rivera   I do.

Hernandez   Well, in the late 1800s thousands of cattle and lots of cowboys took the trail from here to the railroad in Abilene, Kansas. It is estimated that at its peak, in 1871, over 600,000 cattle were driven north to market.

Rivera   That's a lot of beef. And Maria, we have time for just a few words about your beautiful city, San Antonio.

Hernandez   There's so much to tell, but let me mention our beautiful River Walk. The San Antonio River flows through the city and it is lined with trees, cafes, shops, and galleries. It's a great place for lunch or dinner — or even a boat ride on the river. I think San Antonio is the best of two worlds— Mexican and American. Over half of the city's residents have Mexican roots, and I think I can say that time does heal wounds, and today there are countless friendships across our borders.

Rivera   Thank you, Maria, and thank you, all our guests, callers and emailers for being part of another segment of *All Around America.* Next we are off to New Orleans, Louisiana, where we'll experience the French influence in this country of ours. You won't want to miss that! And now let's have a few more calls from our listening audience.

New Orleans
A Cultural Mélange

The French Quarter

New Orleans is a unique city. It is a wonderful mix of people: Spanish, French, French Canadians (Cajuns), African Americans, Native Americans, and others. Every year there is a great celebration in New Orleans called Mardi Gras. The city is famous for its music and its food.

Michelle

Time Travelers

J D Rivera, Talk Show Host
Michelle Duvalier, Guide
Mayor, New Orleans
Paul Bouchard, Famous Chef
Louis Armstrong, Jazz Great
Caller from Las Vegas, Nevada
Caller from Hartford, Connecticut

New Orleans

Louis Armstrong

Rivera Good morning, everyone, and welcome to *All Around America,* the radio talk show that takes you to unique and interesting places in this great country of ours. And do we have a show for you today! We are in one of the most interesting cities in the U.S., New Orleans, Louisiana. But before we take our calls, let me introduce our guide, Michelle Duvalier. Welcome to the show, Michelle.

Duvalier Glad to be here. And welcome to a very special city, that is to say, it's unique.

Rivera So, why is it so special?

Duvalier Well, first of all, I think it's the people. You've got a wonderful ethnic mix of people: French and Spanish descendants, African-Americans, Cajuns, as well as a Native American population. Of course, we have many others, too, like the Italian, Irish, and Latinos. This gives the city an exotic feel of being European, yet Southern at the same time. Then, of course, there are wonderful, unusual places to visit.

Rivera Interesting! So, let's go to the phones. I know our listeners will want to know all about it. From Las Vegas, Nevada, you're on the air!

Las Vegas Interesting program, J D. Somebody told me that Mardi Gras is the greatest party in the country. I've heard so much about this Mardi Gras. What's so great about it, anyway? Here in Las Vegas, we have a party every night.

Rivera Want to take this call, your honor? Folks, let me first introduce you to the mayor of New Orleans. Glad you could come, and welcome to the show.

Mayor Glad to be here, and welcome to our great city. Mardi Gras, that's what we're known for. It means "Fat Tuesday," in French. It's the day before Lent, the Christian Days of fasting — 40 days before Easter. It's probably America's biggest festival with over a million people coming to the city from all over the world. The city really puts on a show then. As a matter of fact, we call Mardi Gras the greatest free show on Earth. There are spectacular parades, music, and dancing. People really let loose. Mardi Gras is one giant party.

Las Vegas How long does it last?

Mayor Well, officially it starts the Friday before Fat Tuesday, but it seems that it's starting earlier and earlier. Parties get going months before.

Rivera So, if you folks like to party, this is the place to be. We have an emailer from Charlotte, North Carolina, who asks, "I've heard a lot about the food in New Orleans, and I'm interested in cooking. Is the food there really so special?"

New Orleans

Duvalier You're in luck, Charlotte, because we have with us one of the world's finest chefs, Paul Bouchard. Paul, tell the folks about the great food we have here.

Bouchard I'd love to. New Orleans is a gourmet's paradise. We are known especially for our Creole and Cajun dishes. A famous Creole dish is shrimp or crawfish over rice, and a Cajun one is gumbo, the thick soup made with okra, seafood, chicken, sausage, and rice. And everybody loves our beignets, those delicious warm square donuts with powdered sugar. Great with coffee.

Rivera Stop! You're making me hungry! But, Paul, tell us what do Creole and Cajun mean? I think our listeners would like to know.

Bouchard Creole refers to the descendants of the French and Spanish. Generally, Creole cooking has rich sauces and many spices. It's very elegant. Cajun refers to Acadians, French Canadians who were forced to leave Nova Scotia in the 1700s. Their food is usually spicy. If you love to eat, this is the place to be.

Rivera Fascinating! Now a call from Hartford, Connecticut. Go ahead.

Hartford Thanks for taking my call. Is there any chance of talking to Louie Armstrong, the jazz great? He's from New Orleans where jazz was born, right?

Rivera Right. Satchmo, want to take this call?

Armstrong It'd be my pleasure. What's your question, Hartford?

Hartford First, Mr. Armstrong, it's such a privilege talking to you.

Armstrong   Please, please, none of that "Mister" stuff. Just, call me Satchmo.

Hartford   Okay, Satchmo. I just want to say that my parents remember dancing to your band in New York way back in the '50s. They've got all your records, too. They say you were the best ever.

Armstrong   Well, thank you. I think we were great. We did gigs in almost every major city in the U.S., in Africa, Asia, Europe and South America, too. It was great. The people just mobbed us. We had a ball.

Duvalier   In my opinion, this man is a real American icon. The sweet, original jazz sounds he created with his trumpet are unsurpassed.

Hartford   Mr. Arm — er, Satchmo, how did you get started with jazz and all that? I mean, did your family give you music lessons?

Armstrong   Oh, no. My family was very poor, and we lived in a very rough neighborhood. I quit school after the third grade to go to work just to keep the family going. I actually learned to play in a home for boys, but once I got out, I was hooked on music. I loved playing that horn. I played on the riverboats coming down the Mississippi. That's how I got my start.

Mayor   May I jump in here? I think the city of New Orleans owes you an apology, Satchmo. At one time some folks in this town didn't want you playing here because your band was integrated. Can you believe that! Of all the stupidity!

Armstrong   Hard to believe, but it happened.

New Orleans

Duvalier May I just add that for all the jazz lovers of the world, you can hear jazz being played on almost any corner of the city. And, of course, for a real live concert, you can't beat Preservation Hall with a concert every single night.

Rivera Michelle, before we call it quits, tell us some other places we absolutely shouldn't miss in this great city.

Duvalier Well, don't pass up the chance to see the historic French Quarter with its wonderful old world architecture, the Garden District with its beautiful trees and flowers, and of course, the great restaurants, just to mention a few. Just walking around and getting the feel of the city is a great experience, too. And that's free.

Rivera So listeners, it's time to leave this unique city on the Mississippi. If we had time, we'd take a boat down to the mouth of the river, across the Gulf of Mexico and then up the east coast of Florida to our next stop, the Kennedy Space Center. But, let's keep the lines open for a few more calls.

Street Buskers on Royal Street

Kennedy Space Center

The Exploration of Space

Rocket Tour at the Space Center

Space Shuttle Launch

The Kennedy Space Center is on Cape Canaveral in Florida. Over 3,000 spacecraft have been launched from the center. The First American astronaut in space was Alan Shepard. John Glenn was the first American to orbit the earth, and Neil Armstrong was the first man to step on the moon.

Mary

Time Travelers

J D Rivera, Talk Show Host
Mary Sikorski, Guide
John Glenn, Astronaut
Alan B. Shepard, Jr., Astronaut
Neil Armstrong, Astronaut
Caller from Charleston,
    West Virginia
Caller from Baltimore, Maryland

The Kennedy Space Center

John Glenn

Alan Shepard

Neil Armstrong

Rivera Good morning, everyone, and welcome to *All Around America,* the talk show that takes you to interesting places in this great country and lets you talk to famous people. Well, here we are at the Kennedy Space Center in Cape Canaveral, Florida, where you'll be talking to a few of America's astronauts. With us is our guide, Mary Sikorksi. Mary, this place is huge. How big is it, anyway?

Sikorski Well, as you can see, it includes many huge buildings. For example, one of the largest in the world is the Vehicle Assembly Building where spacecraft like the shuttle are put together. Then, there are the launching pads from which the spacecraft take off, and the NASA Launch Operations center, the brains of the place. It's really like a small city for space travel.

Rivera Mary, you mentioned the shuttle. Can you explain what that is?

Sikorski Sure. The shuttle is a vehicle that looks like an airplane. It's called a shuttle because after it is launched, it can return and be used again. It can shuttle back and forth between earth and space stations.

Rivera   Thanks. Now, let's go to the phones. I know our listeners have lots of questions. Charleston, West Virginia, go ahead.

Charleston   Thanks, J D. Mary, can you give us a little history of this place? When did it all begin?

Sikorski   The construction began in 1950 when America got into the Space Age. And since that time, over 3,000 spacecraft have been launched from here.

Charleston   Wow! That many!

Sikorski   Right. The first rocket was launched in 1950, and the first satellite, Explorer I, was launched in '58. The first manned space flight in '61.

Charleston   Maybe we can even talk to some of our astronauts who flew those missions.

Rivera   They're on the line. Let's hear first from Alan Shepard.

Shepard   Good morning! This is Alan Shepard.

Rivera   Alan! Welcome to the show!

Charleston   You were actually America's first man in space, weren't you?

Shepard   That's right! I had that privilege as part of the Mercury Program to put a man in space. Although I was in space for only fifteen minutes, I felt history was being made.

Sikorski   And that was on May 5, 1961. I remember all of us being glued to the TV on that day. It was a long fifteen minutes. We sure were happy when you returned.

Rivera   Let's see who our next caller is.

The Kennedy Space Center

Glenn   Hello, this is John Glenn.

Rivera   John, good to hear from you! You were America's first man to orbit the earth, weren't you?

Glenn   Yes, yes I was. And what a thrill it was! I orbited the earth three times in less than five hours. It was a truly amazing day, February 20, 1962 — I'll never forget it. Of course, as you know, I went up later for a space flight as a senior citizen in 1990.

Rivera   Yes, I remember that. By then, space travel was much easier. And now a caller from Columbus, Ohio. You're on the air.

Armstrong   This is Neil Armstrong.

Rivera   Neil, first man on the moon! Welcome to the show!

Armstrong   Thank you, glad to be here, and ready to answer any questions.

Rivera   Well, here's one from Baltimore, Maryland.

Baltimore   I'd like to talk to Neil Armstrong. Mr. Armstrong?

Armstrong   Call me Neil.

Baltimore   Neil, what was it like to actually take that first step on the moon?

Armstrong   It was a tremendous experience. Climbing down that ladder and putting my foot on the moon was awesome. I felt I was doing it not only for myself, but also for all mankind. But I want to tell you that looking from the moon at the earth was awesome, too. It sure made me feel humble.

Baltimore I have another question for whoever wants to answer it.

Rivera Go ahead, caller. What's your question?

Baltimore Do you really think we should be going up in space? I mean, with all the problems right here on earth — poverty, disease, pollution — wouldn't we be better off spending money to solve those problems, to say nothing of the cost in lives and money of the space disasters that happen?

Rivera Excellent question, who wants to take this one on?

Glenn I'll answer that.

Armstrong So will I.

Shepard Let me get in on that, too.

Rivera Go ahead, guys.

Glenn Well, first of all, I don't think space exploration can be stopped. It's in human nature to explore. From the very beginning, we have pushed our boundaries. I don't think we humans will ever stop wondering about what's on this earth, under the sea, or in space.

Armstrong Right on, John! And think how much space travel adds to our knowledge and understanding of the universe, actually about us humans ourselves and our role here on earth. It's pretty heady stuff.

Shepard Let me add something, too. Who knows, someday, maybe humans will live in space. I know that sounds far-fetched, but even as recently as 100 years ago, people thought it was impossible to fly. Can space travel be far behind?

The Kennedy Space Center

Armstrong And don't forget, further discoveries that we make in space may also someday be used right here on earth. For example, our travel in space has already given us a better understanding of diseases and medical problems. These are important contributions.

Rivera I guess, caller, you could say these guys are all for space exploration despite the risks. But, we certainly can't take space travel for granted or be careless, can we?

Armstrong Absolutely, not! I think we can all see eye to eye on that.

Rivera Now, an email from Kathy in Topeka, Kansas. She asks if she can actually go and see a launch.

Sikorski Absolutely! Just check out the website for the information on visiting and watching launches.

Rivera Well, there you have it, folks! Who knows? Maybe someday, you, too, will travel and explore in space. That's it for now. See you next week when we drive up the Florida coast and learn about the exploration of the old New World. We'll be in Saint Augustine, Florida. Before we pack up here on Cape Canaveral, there is time for a few more calls.

International Space Station

The Castillo de San Marcos

Spain in the New World

The Bastion

Juan Ponce de León was an early explorer who claimed Florida for Spain. The Spanish wanted to protect their land in the New World so they built the Castillo de San Marcos in North Florida. It is one of the oldest buildings in America. The Castillo was used as a prison by the American government before it was finally closed.

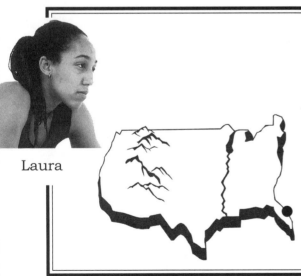

Laura

Time Travelers

J D Rivera, Talk Show Host
Laura Rodriguez,
    National Park Service Guide
Juan Ponce de León,
    Spanish Explorer
Bernardo de Galvez,
    Governor of Louisiana
Caller from Columbia,
    South Carolina
Caller from Providence, Rhode Island
Caller from Cheyenne, Wyoming

The Castillo de San Marcos

Juan Ponce de León

Bernardo de Galvez

Rivera Welcome once again to *All Around America, The Time Traveler's Talk Show.* Our last program at the Kennedy Space Center was all about exploration — the exploration of space. And today we will go back in time to an earlier exploration, earlier even than Lewis and Clark's exploration of the American West. We're in Saint Augustine, Florida, where we'll learn about the Spanish exploration and colonization of North America. With us is our guide for today, Laura Rodriguez. Welcome, Laura.

Rodriguez Thanks, J D. We are standing atop of one of the walls of the Castillo de San Marcos. This star-shaped fort is one of the oldest buildings in North America. It was built by Spain between the years 1672 and 1695.

Rivera So this fort is over 300 years old. Why did the Spanish build it, and why here?

Rodriguez Well, J D, to understand that, we have to go back even further in time. You know, of course, that Columbus reached the New World in 1492, and that was the beginning of a long struggle among several European nations to explore and colonize the New World. Among the early explorers was Juan Ponce de León.

Rivera   And we've asked him to spend some time with us today. Welcome to the show, Señor Ponce de León.

de León   Gracias, J D, and hola, Maria. Columbus opened a big door for us Spaniards. I came with him on his second voyage.

Rivera   So you knew Columbus, personally.

de León   Indeed. We spent many hours together across the Atlantic. A few years later, I came back to claim Puerto Rico for Spain, and I was the governor there for three years. In 1513 I sailed north to explore this area and landed near here.

Rivera   And . . .

de León   And I realized immediately that Spain should have this land, too. It was beautiful. I named it Florida.

Rivera   And so today, it is still Florida. Thank you very much for being with us today, Juan.

Rodriguez   I might mention, J D, that Ponce de León came back again, hoping to establish a colony here. And there is a legend that he believed that near here was a fountain of youth. If you drank from it, you would become young again. But unfortunately, he was killed in a battle with the Timucuan Indians, who considered this part of the world to be theirs. He discovered death instead of youth.

Rivera   We have a caller from Columbia, South Carolina, on the line. Go ahead, Columbia.

Columbia   Hello everybody. Here's my question: the Spanish did eventually take control of Florida, didn't they?

The Castillo de San Marcos

Rodriguez   They did, and not just Florida. Throughout the 1500s and 1600s, the Spanish established a huge empire in the New World, from California to Chile.

Columbia   So when and why was this fort built?

Rodriguez   As I mentioned, the Spanish, English, French, Portuguese, and Dutch were all trying to establish colonies, and just north of Saint Augustine, the French and English were too close for comfort. So the Castillo was begun in 1672 to help protect Spain's possessions in this part of the New World.

Rivera   Excuse me, Laura, we have a question from a caller in Providence, Rhode Island.

Providence   I stopped in at the fort a few years ago, and I remember that the Spanish lost the fort to the English. How did that happen?

Rodriguez   Well, at the end of the Seven Years' War (known as the French and Indian War in North America), England came out on top, and Spain gave up the Gulf Coast and North Florida.

Providence   But I seem to remember that Spain got the fort back again, how did that happen?

Rivera   Let me interrupt here. I have someone on the line who can tell us about that. Are you there, sir, and can you tell us who you are and what happened?

Galvez   I am Bernardo de Galvez, and I was the governor of Spanish Louisiana. We Spaniards were very happy to see the American colonies to the north go to war against our great rival England in 1775.

Providence   And so how are you involved with this story?

Galvez Well, I never actually got to the Castillo, but in 1779, Spain declared war on England. I attacked the British forts all along the Gulf Coast, including Pensacola in north Florida, and tied up many British soldiers and supplies that could have been used against the Americans.

Rodriguez And because of that, we Americans should thank Señor Galvez as a hero of the American Revolution. Without his successful attacks, the American struggle against England would have been a great deal more difficult.

Galvez I think so, and anyway, the British had to return the Castillo to us in 1784 when the Americans were victorious. Thank you, J D, for having me on the program.

Rodriguez And let me add, J D, that when you go to Washington, D. C., look for a statue of Señor Galvez at Virginia and 22nd Street. And in fact, the grateful Americans named a city for him, Galveston, Texas.

Rivera Thank you so much, Señor Galvez, for being with us today. And now we have a caller from Cheyenne, Wyoming. Go ahead Cheyenne.

Cheyenne I'm interested in the history of our Native Americans, and I believe many were imprisoned in the Castillo. Is that right?

Rodriguez It is indeed. That happened after the Americans bought Florida from Spain and took over the fort.

Cheyenne And that was in 1821?

Rodriguez Exactly. The Seminole Indians of Florida were not happy with the settlers who were taking over their homeland. There was a war, and some of the Indians, including their chief, Osceola, were locked up in the Castillo, which the Americans had renamed Fort Marion.

The Castillo de San Marcos

Cheyenne   Was Florida a state at that time?

Rodriguez   It became a state in 1845, but shortly afterwards, it joined the Confederate States of America in the Civil War against the North. However, the fort was very lightly defended and it fell to a northern gunboat. The ship took the fort and the city without firing a shot.

Cheyenne   And what was the final page in the history of the fort?

Rodriguez   Basically, it became a prison, and once again for Native Americans. As you know, many American Indian tribes fought against the invasion of the land they considered home. In 1886, about 450 Apache Indians were imprisoned here and in Fort Pickens, in Pensacola, Florida.

Rivera   So what happened to them?

Rodriguez   Eventually they were let go. Shortly after that, the fort was closed. It became a national monument in 1924, and in 1942, it was once again named "Castillo de San Marcos," in honor of its Spanish heritage.

Rivera   The walls of this fort have seen a long, complicated, and fascinating story, and five different flags have flown here. There's much more to tell, but we're running out of time. We now have to pack up our mobile studio and head north to D.C. Thank you, Laura, and thanks to our guests and callers, but before we hit the road, let's take a few more calls from our listeners.

Washington, D.C.

A City of Memorials and Monuments

The White House

The capital of the United States is Washington, D.C. It is a city of many monuments. The White House is the president's home. The Washington Monument and the Lincoln Memorial are very popular with visitors. One of the newest memorials is the Vietnam War Memorial.

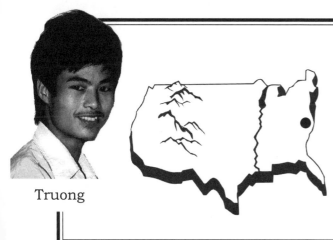

Truong

Time Travelers:

J D Rivera, Talk Show Host
Truong Nguyen, Guide
The President
Dolley Madison,
    Wife of fourth U.S. president
Maya Ying Lin,
    Architect of Vietnam Memorial
Caller from Little Rock, Arkansas
Caller from Fargo, North Dakota

Washington, D.C.

Dolley Madison

Maya Ying Lin

Rivera   Good morning and welcome to *All Around America, The Time Traveler's Talk Show* that takes you to historic places across the nation. Today we wind up our tour of America at a place where history is made every day — Washington, our nation's capital in the District of Columbia. The district is not a state. It is a federal district of 67 square miles. And we're at the White House. With us is our guide, Truong Nguyen, who will take us on a sightseeing tour of this beautiful White House and the city. Welcome to the show. Truong, ready to go?

Nguyen   Thanks, J D. Ready when you are. Let's start right here at The White House.

Rivera   Let's go. Look! Is that the President going into the Oval Office?

Nguyen   That's the President all right.

Rivera   I wonder whether she'd be willing to talk to us. Madame President?

President   Yes?

All Around America

Rivera   Madame President, I'm J D Rivera and we're doing the radio show *All Around America.* Perhaps you've heard of it? Our show is visiting historical places, and here in the District of Columbia, the White House is first on our list. It would be such an honor to have you on our show. Would you have time to say a few words to our listeners?

President   I'd be glad to. I've actually heard a few of your shows, J D. Right now, I'm waiting for the Ambassador from Spain. As you know, the White House is a symbol of democracy. This house belongs to all Americans. I'm just a tenant here. The American people are my landlord. So, look around and enjoy this beautiful home. But, excuse me, there's the Ambassador now.

Rivera   Thank you, Madame President. Truong, what a scoop that was! Did you set that up?

Nguyen   No way, J D. That was pure luck.

Rivera   Well, phew, on with the show! Here's an email from Milwaukee, Wisconsin that asks "Is it true that the White House actually burned down at one time?"

Nguyen   I think First Lady, Dolley Madison, can answer that. She was there.

Rivera   Dolley Madison, wife of our fourth president, welcome to our show.

Madison   May I say, I am delighted to be on your show. Yes, the White House was burned when the British invaded Washington in 1814. It was awful! I was there minutes before it happened! But fortunately, it didn't burn down, although it was badly damaged.

Rivera   What exactly happened?

Washington, D.C.

Madison   Well, the President was away. We could hear the cannons in the distance, so I knew the British were near. I got a message from the President to leave at once. But I was determined to pack some documents and the portrait of George Washington first. That portrait that you see hanging over there is the exact one we managed to save that day. I'm especially proud of it.

Rivera   Quite a story, Dolley! You were one brave lady. And speaking of George Washington, let's go over to the Washington Monument.

Nguyen   Good idea. That beautiful monument is, of course, a tribute to our first president. He was so loved and respected that people wanted a monument built for him during his lifetime, but he wouldn't hear of it. So they didn't start building it until after he died. The monument is 555 feet high and can be seen from almost anywhere in the city.

Rivera   Now, let's go to the phones. The board is all lit up with calls waiting, so let's get to our first caller. Caller from Little Rock, Arkansas, you're on the air.

Little Rock   Thanks. I visited Washington, D. C., a few years ago with my family and we climbed the 898 steps to get to the top of the Washington Monument. And the view from the top was really something!

Rivera   It is indeed impressive. What else did you see on your visit?

Little Rock   We saw the Lincoln Memorial.

Rivera   That's my favorite. Truong, can you tell us a little about it?

106

Nguyen Well, the Lincoln Memorial is a massive marble building, 188 feet long and 118 feet wide, dedicated to Abraham Lincoln. Tourists often come here first when visiting Washington.

Little Rock We did come here first because my dad wanted to see it again.

Rivera Why was that?

Little Rock Dad was active in the Civil Rights Movement. In 1963 he took part in the March on Washington, and he heard Martin Luther King give his magnificent "I Have a Dream" speech at the Lincoln Memorial. In my view, 1963 was the turning point for Black America. We've made a lot of progress toward that famous statement in the Declaration of Independence: "All men are created equal." But there's still work to do.

Rivera Little Rock, thank you for your call. As we reach the end of our journey around this nation, your reminder is well taken. There is indeed still work to be done. And, folks, as you can see, Washington, D. C., is a place where history is made and history comes alive. What shall we visit next, Truong?

Nguyen What about going over to the Vietnam Memorial? That's really special. And of course it has a special meaning for me.

Rivera Now, that's one place I've always wanted to see. And while we're going over there, let's take a call. Fargo, North Dakota, go ahead.

Fargo I'd like to speak to the architect of the Vietnam Memorial.

Washington, D.C.

Rivera Maya, this one's for you. Listeners, let me introduce Maya Ying Lin, architect of the Vietnam Memorial. It's a pleasure to have you here, Maya.

Lin Pleasure to be here.

Fargo Maya, can you tell us a little bit about the design of the Memorial?

Lin First of all, this memorial is very, very simple. It's basically a huge slab of black granite wall cut into the hillside.

Fargo So, what makes it so special?

Lin I think it's all of the names of the men and women who died in the Vietnam War. Each and every name is carved right into the wall. I wanted a memorial that would honor these men and women by remembering their names.

Rivera As we look around, we can see people looking for names of their loved ones, and then tracing the names with their fingers. It's very moving. Maya, you created a wonderful tribute to their sacrifice.

Lin Thank you.

Nguyen I should also point out, J D , that right across from us on the mall is the Korean War Memorial, and between the Washington and Lincoln Memorials is the World War II Memorial.

Rivera Truong, our time is almost up.

Nguyen Oh, no! We haven't even mentioned the Smithsonian Institute and the National Air and Space Museum, the National Gallery of Art....

All Around America

Rivera   Truong, there's too much to see here in Washington, D.C., and just not enough time for us to describe it all. We have barely scratched the surface. So, listeners, come for a visit and see for yourself. Thank you guests, and thank you callers. And here in Washington, our journey and our program comes to a close. I've enjoyed every minute, and I hope all you listeners out there have enjoyed it, too. Before we sign off, there's still time for a few questions and comments about our nation's capital.

U.S. Capitol Building in the Spring, Washington, D.C.

The Jefferson Memorial
Washington, D.C.

The Spanish fort at
Matanzas inlet –
Florida

Fact Sheets

Statue of Liberty _{page 1}

1. The Statue of Liberty is located on Liberty Island. *where*

2. The statue was a gift of friendship from France. *why*

3. It celebrated the friendship established between France and America during America's Revolutionary War. *what*

4. The statue arrived in hundreds of boxes on a French ship in 1885. *how*

5. The statue was dedicated on October 28, 1886. *when*

6. The statue was established as a National Monument on October 15, 1924. *when*

7. Ellis Island became part of the Statue of Liberty National Monument on May 11, 1965. *when*

8. Ellis Island was the entry point for approximately 12 million immigrants. *what, how many*

9. Ellis Island operated from 1892 - 1954. *how long*

10. The statue is 151 feet from its toe to the top of the torch. *how tall*

11. There are 192 steps to the top of the pedestal. *how many*

12. There are 354 steps from the bottom of the pedestal to the crown. *how many*

13. There are 25 windows in the crown. *how many*

14. Lady Liberty holds a tablet that says "July 4, 1776." *what*

15. The title of Emma Lazarus' poem is "The New Colossus." *what*

16. The colossus refers to one of the Seven Wonders of the World, the Colossus of Rhodes. *what, where*

17. The statue can be reached by ferry from two places: Battery Park in New York City or Liberty State Park in Jersey City. *how*

18. Bartholdi also did a statue of Lafayette in Union Square in New York City. *what else*

19. Lafayette was a French nobleman who fought with the Americans during the Revolutionary War. *who*

20. Bartholdi created a statue of Lafayette and Washington at the Place des Etats-Unis in Paris. *what, where*

The Boston Freedom Trail _{page 7}

1. Boston is the capital of the state of Massachusetts.

2. Boston is the largest city in New England.

3. The population of Boston (2000 census)is 589,141.

4. The largest ethnic groups in Boston are Irish and Italian.

5. Boston was settled in 1630.

6. At the Boston Tea Party, the patriots dumped 342 chests of tea into the water.

7. Paul Revere was a well-known silversmith.

8. Samuel Adams was second cousin to John Adams. His father owned a brewery.

9. John Adams and John Quincy Adams both graduated from Harvard College.

10. The Battle of Bunker Hill was actually fought on Breed's Hill.

11. The first shots of the Revolution were fired at Lexington.

12. At Breed's Hill, the British were commanded by General William Howe.

13. At Breed's Hill, the militia was commanded by Colonel Prescott and General Putnam.

14. Harvard University is the oldest institution of higher learning in the United States.

Fact Sheets

15. Harvard University and the Massachusetts Institute of Technology are located in Cambridge.

16. Cambridge is across the Charles River from Boston.

17. Boston Latin School was the first public school in America. It was established in 1635.

18. There are more than 50 institutions of higher learning in metropolitan Boston.

19. The Boston Public Library was opened in 1854. It was the first free public library in America.

Lowell National Historical Park page 13

1. The population of Lowell (2000 census) is 105,167.

2. The famous American painter James McNeill Whistler was born in Lowell.

3. One of Lowell's earliest ethnic neighborhood is called "the Acre."

4. In the early 1900s, the residents of the Acre were primarily Irish and Greek.

5. The first inhabitants of the area around Lowell were Pennacook Indians.

6. In the 17th century, many Pennacook Indians died from disease.

7. By 1725, the Pennacooks had left the Lowell area and moved to Canada.

6. The source of the Merrimack River is the lakes and mountains of New Hampshire.

7. The Pawtucket Falls were 32 feet high.

8. The Merrimack was very polluted until the 1970's. Nowadays, the quality of the water is improving.

9. A working turbine and power loom demonstrate the use of water power at the Suffolk Mills Turbine exhibit.

10. A restored boardinghouse can be visited at the Working People Exhibit.

11. At the Boott Cotton Mills, there were eight rows of boardinghouses.

12. Each row of boardinghouses contained four units for unmarried workers, and one unit for married workers and families.

13. Most of the Mill Girls were 15-30 years old.

14. In the late 19th century, women held almost two-thirds of the textile jobs.

15. Sarah Bagley was born on a New Hampshire farm. She edited a labor newspaper called "The Voice of Industry."

16. Jack Kerouac wrote more than 20 books before he died in St. Petersburg, Florida in 1969 at the age of 47.

Gettysburg, Pennsylvania page 19

1. The population of Gettysburg (2000 census) is 7,490.

2. The Historical Park covers 3,400 acres (1,380 hectares).

3. The Eisenhower National Historic Site is also in Gettysburg. It was the home of General and President Dwight Eisenhower.

4. Lee's army was about 75,000 men. There were about 90,000 men in the Union Army.

5. The commander of the Union Army was General George G. Meade.

6. On July 1, the Confederate Army pushed the Union Army back. The Union Army retreated through the town of Gettysburg. They took up new positions south of the town.

7. The Union's new positions were on Cemetery Hill and Culp's Hill.

8. On July 2, the Confederates attacked the Union positions on the hills.

9. The Confederate attack on the hills was defeated.

10. On July 3, General George Pickett led a charge against the Union army.

11. Pickett began his charge with 15,000 men. His attack failed, and he lost 10,000 men.

12. After Pickett's defeat, the Confederate Army began to retreat.

13. Over 7,000 men died at the Battle of Gettysburg.

14. In the same week, the Union Army won a battle at Vicksburg, Mississippi.

15. The Union commander at Vicksburg was Ulysses S. Grant. He became the 18th president of the United States.

16. After the battles of Gettysburg and Vicksburg, the South was mostly on the defensive.

17. The Civil War ended on April 9, 1865. Five days later, President Lincoln was killed by an assassin.

11. After the Great fire, Chicago created one of the world's first modern fire departments.

12. At the turn of the twentieth century, thousands of European immigrants came to Chicago.

13. The first passenger elevator was invented by Elisha Otis. It was installed in a New York store in 1857.

14. Louis Sullivan was born in 1856 in Boston. He died in 1924 in Chicago. He was poor and almost unknown when he died.

13. The most outstanding American architect of the 20th Century is probably Frank Lloyd Wright. He began his career working for Louis Sullivan.

14. Frank Lloyd Wright's book "Genius and Mobocracy" was a tribute to Sullivan.

Chicago, Illinois page 25

1. The population of Chicago (2000 census) is 2,896,016.

2. Chicago is the third largest city in the U.S.

3. The name of the downtown center of Chicago is the Loop.

4. An elevated train circles the city center. The train is called the El. The train makes a loop around the city center.

5. The Erie Canal in New York opened trade from the East through the Great Lakes.

6. There are five Great Lakes: Ontario, Erie, Huron, Michigan, and Superior.

7. Chicago became an important port on Lake Michigan.

8. Chicago is a natural transportation center. Many trains go in and out of Chicago. O'Hare International Airport is the second busiest in the world. A canal links Chicago to the Mississippi River.

9. Chicago is a major market for grain (corn, wheat) and livestock (cattle, pigs).

10. In 1979 Jane Byrne became Chicago's first woman mayor, and in 1983, Harold Washington became its first Black mayor.

St. Louis page 31

1. The population of St. Louis (2000 census) is 348,189.

2. St. Louis was founded by the French in 1764 as a fur trading post.

3. It was acquired by the U.S. in 1803 as part of the Louisiana Purchase.

4. The Missouri River joins the Mississippi River just north of St. Louis.

5. Meriwether Lewis was President Jefferson's private secretary from 1801-1803.

6. While Lewis served as Jefferson's secretary, he planned the famous expedition.

7. When Lewis returned he was appointed governor of Louisiana Territory.

8. Lewis died in 1809. Many think he was either murdered or a suicide.

9. William Clark died in 1838, at the age of 68.

10. After Lewis' death, Clark published the records of the famous journey.

11. The expedition spent its first winter in South Dakota at a Mandan Indian village.

12. On the return trip, Lewis and Clark split up. Lewis followed the Missouri River and Clark followed the Yellowstone River to North Dakota.

13. On the return, Sacagawea stayed with the Wind River Shoshone people in Wyoming.

14. Saarinen also designed the CBS building in New York City.

Mount Rushmore
page 37

1. The state of South Dakota is 46th in population: 756,600.

2. The major immigrants to South Dakota were from Germany, Norway, Sweden, and Denmark.

3. The original people of South Dakota were the Mandan, Hidatsa, Arikara, and Sioux Indians.

4. Washington was the 1st president, Jefferson, the 3rd, Lincoln the 16th, Theodore Roosevelt the 39th.

5. The last of the four heads to be completed was Roosevelt.

6. The sculpture took 14 years.

7. Gutzon Borglum also did the head of Lincoln in the national capitol.

8. Borglum was born in Idaho in 1871.

9. In 1916, Borglum started work on a Confederate memorial on the side of Stone Mountain in Georgia. The work stopped in 1925 and started again in 1963. The sculpture was completed in 1970.

10. The Black Hills are called black because of the dark pine trees on the sides of the mountains.

11. The largest gold mine in the U.S. is the Homestake Mine in the Black Hills.

12. The Badlands National Park is about 60 miles east of Rushmore.

13. Wounded Knee Massacre Historical Site is just south of the Badlands. The last major fight between Native Americans and the U.S. Army was at Wounded Knee in 1890. 300 Lakota Sioux were killed.

The Oregon Trail
page 43

1. The first settler to make the entire trip with a family was Joel Walker in 1840.

2. In 1843, the first large wagon train of over 800 people with 120 wagons made the trip.

3. Gold was discovered in California in 1848, and many people traveled part of the Oregon Trail to California.

4. In southern Idaho, a branch of the trail went to California.

5. In 1978, congress named the trail a National Historic Trail.

6. Most settlers finished the journey on rafts on the Columbia River.

7. By the 1860's, travel to Oregon began to decrease.

8. The trail follows the Platte and North Platte Rivers through Nebraska and Wyoming.

9. The South Pass is 7550 feet in elevation.

10. The Continental Divide separates the rivers of the continent. East of the divide the rivers flow to the Atlantic. West of the divide the rivers flow to the Pacific.

11. In Idaho, the trail follows the Snake River.

12. Baker City was once the largest city in Oregon.

13. The Columbia River forms part of the boundary between Oregon and Washington.

14. The Columbia River was discovered by a Boston trader, Robert Gray, in 1792. He named the river after his ship.

15. The Whitmans were Presbyterian missionaries.

16. The Whitman mission became an important stop for travelers on the trail.

17. The name "Walla Walla" is from the Cayuse Indian language.

Fact Sheets

Alaska page 49

1. Vitus Bering was from Denmark, but he was employed by the Czar of Russia.

2. 10,000 years ago, there was a land bridge from Asia to Alaska.

3. The long string of islands that extend into the sea are called the Aleutian Islands.

4. In World War II, Japan occupied two of the Aleutian Islands.

5. Alaska is four times bigger than Texas.

6. The largest national park in Alaska is the Wrangell-St. Elias Park.

7. Mt. McKinley is 20,320 feet high.

8. William McKinley was the 25th president of the United States.

9. The longest river in Alaska is the Yukon.

10. The Yukon River is 1,265 miles long.

11. The southeastern coast of Alaska is called the "Panhandle."

12. The capital of Alaska is Juneau. It is located in the panhandle.

13. The largest city in Alaska is Anchorage.

14. The population of Anchorage is a little over a quarter of a million.

15. There are large deposits of oil and gas on the Arctic Coastal Plain.

16. A pipeline carries the petroleum to the port of Valdez.

17. The Trans-Alaska Pipeline is 1,287 kilometers long — about 800 miles.

18. Alaska's fishing industry is the largest of all the states.

19. The most important fish is salmon.

20. Alaska became a state in 1959.

Hawaii page 55

1. The population of Hawaii is 1,224,398. It is 42nd.

2. Hawaii is 43rd in size (area).

3. Hawaii is about 2,400 miles southwest of San Francisco.

4. The capital and largest city is Honolulu.

5. The chief industry is tourism.

6. Hawaii is called the aloha state. *Aloha* means something like love or goodwill in Hawaiian.

7. There are about 130 islands in the state.

8. Mauna Kea is the highest point, 13,796 feet high.

9. The largest of the eight major islands is Hawaii; the smallest is Niihau.

10. Niihau is a private island. It is not possible to visit it.

11. Pearl Harbor is the site of the Japanese attack on the United States on December 7, 1941.

12. Almost 1,400 different flowering plants are found on Hawaii.

13. About 25% of the population is of Japanese descent. 14% are Filipino, 9% are Hawaiians. The rest are mostly white.

14. Between AD 400 and 900, Polynesians from the Marquesas Islands and Tahiti settled the islands.

15. The Polynesians traveled across the ocean in large canoes.

16. When Captain Cook visited the islands there were about 300,000 Hawaiians.

17. Waikiki is a beautiful beach at Honolulu.

18. Hawaii Volcanoes National park is on Hawaii.

Fact Sheets

The Golden Gate Bridge page 61

1. The Goden Gate Bridge is 1.7 miles long.

2. The center of the bridge is 220 feet above the water.

3. The bridge attracts many suicides. On average, one every two weeks.

4. The bridge was the longest suspension bridge in the world until 1964 when the Verrazano-Narrows Bridge in New York was finished.

5. California is the largest state in population. (2000) census: 33,871,648.

6. San Francisco's population is 776,763.

7. San Francisco became a major city as a result of a gold rush in 1849.

8. The city was destroyed by an earthquake in 1906. The city burned for three days.

9. Another strong earthquake damaged the city in 1989.

10. San Francisco was the birthplace of the United Nations in 1945.

11. The Golden Gate Recreation Area includes several places in and around San Francisco.

12. Muir Woods has many giant redwood trees. Some trees are over 300 feet tall.

13. John Muir was a naturalist who helped preserve America's forests.

14. Alcatraz was a federal prison from 1934-1963.

15. Alcatraz is also called "The Rock."

16. Alcatraz can be visited by ferry.

17. Chinatown is one of the largest Chinese communities outside Asia.

18. The city of Oakland is across the bay from San Francisco.

The Grand Canyon page 67

1. Arizona is the sixth largest state in area.

2. Arizona is one of the fastest growing states in population. Between 1990 and 2000 the population increased 40%.

3. There are about 20 Indian reservations in the state.

4. Arizona became a state in 1912. It was the 48th state.

5. The largest city in Arizona is Phoenix.

6. The first explorer of Arizona was probably the Spaniard Alvar Nunez Cabeza de Vaca in 1536.

7. As a result of the Mexican War, the U.S. took over most of Arizona from Mexico in 1848.

8. Arizona's border with Mexico is almost 400 miles long.

9. The rock walls of the Grand Canyon represent over a billion years of earth history.

10. Garcia Lopez de Cardenas discovered the canyon in 1540.

11. West of the Canyon, the Hoover Dam on the Colorado River forms Lake Mead.

12. Lake Mead is 115 miles long. A few miles west of Lake Mead is Las Vegas.

13. John Wesley Powell became interested in Indian languages and developed a system for classifying them.

14. The John Wesley Powell Memorial Museum is in Page, Arizona. Page is just north of the canyon and south of Lake Powell.

15. Powell joined the Union Army as a lieutenant of artillery.

16. Powell lost his arm during the Civil War, at the Battle of Shiloh in Tennessee in 1862.

17. Powell was 35 when he went down the Colorado River.

18. Other beautiful natural places in Arizona include the Painted Desert, The Petrified Forest, and Monument Valley.

Fact Sheets

Mesa Verde _{page 73}

1. Colorado is bordered by six states.

2. The state of Colorado is named for the Colorado River. The Colorado River begins in Colorado. Colorado means "red" in Spanish.

3. Colorado has the highest average elevation of all the states. There are more than 1,000 peaks over 10,000 feet.

4. The largest city and capital of Colorado is Denver.

5. There are two national parks in Colorado: Rocky Mountain National Park and Mesa Verde.

6. Mesa Verde is located in southwestern Colorado, about 50 miles from Four Corners.

7. Four Corners is the only place in the U.S. where four states meet at one point. The states are Colorado, New Mexico, Arizona, and Utah.

8. Mesa Verde is 81 square miles in area.

9. Mesa Verde is open to visitors all year.

10. The site was inhabited for nearly 1,000 years.

11. From AD 1-400 the people called Basketmaker II lived on the Mesa. They grew beans, corn and squash and kept dogs and turkeys. They lived in caves and houses dug into the earth.

12. The Basketmaker III people lived to the middle of the 8th century. They introduced pottery and began to build houses.

13. During the Pueblo I and II periods, the people began to build houses of several stories, somewhat like apartment houses.

14. From the 12th to 14th centuries, the people of the Pueblo III period built the cliff dwellings.

15. After the people moved away, the cliff dwellings were forgotten. At the end of the 19th century, cowboys discovered the dwellings. Shortly afterward, archeologists began to preserve the area. The park was established in 1906.

The Alamo _{page 79}

1. Texas is the second largest state in area, after Alaska.

2. San Antonio's population (2000 census) is 1,144,646. It is the 9th largest U.S. city.

3. The Rio Grande River forms the boundary between Texas and Mexico. In Mexico, the river is called Rio Bravo del Norte.

4. The Rio Grande begins in Colorado and flows south through New Mexico to the Texas-Mexico border.

5. The Alamo was established as a Spanish mission in 1718.

6. People of Hispanic origin are about one-third of the population of Texas.

7. The French attempted to establish a presence in Texas in about 1685. The explorer Robert Cavalier, sieur de La Salle was killed by one of his own men in 1687.

8. By the middle of the 18th century, the Spanish controlled the territory of Texas.

9. Mexico became independent from Spain in 1821, and became a republic in 1823.

10. In 1830, the Mexican government passed a law to limit immigration. However, by 1836 the American population of Texas was 50,000.

11. In 1835, war began between the Mexican government and the American settlers (Texans). The Texans captured San Antonio. Texas declared independence in 1836.

12. The Mexican War began in 1846, but fighting ended in 1847 when the Americans occupied Mexico City. Mexico accepted the Rio Grande (Bravo) as the boundary between Texas and Mexico.

13. Mexico also gave up all of the southwest, including California and New Mexico Territory (New Mexico, Arizona, Nevada, Utah, and part of Colorado).

14. In 1845 Texas entered the Union as a slave state and joined the South during the Civil War. However, there were very few battles in Texas. Some fighting occured at the port of Galveston.

117

Fact Sheets

New Orleans page 85

1. New Orleans is the largest city in the state of Louisiana. Its population (2000 census) is 484,674.

2. New Orleans was established by the French in 1718. It was taken over by Spain in 1763. Spain gave it back to France in 1800. It was acquired by the U.S. as part of the Louisiana Purchase of 1803.

3. The Battle of New Orleans was the last battle of the War of 1812 with Britain. It was actually fought in 1815 after the war was over.

4. New Orleans is on the east bank of the Mississippi River. It is actually 110 miles from the mouth of the river.

5. The city is located on a bend in the river. Because of that it is called the "Crescent City." It is also known as "The Big Easy."

6. The land along the Gulf Coast of Louisiana is very low and wet. These wetlands are called the Bayous. Many Cajuns settled in this area.

7. Cajun is a shortened form of "Acadian." Acadia was the name of the land that is now the Canadian province of Nova Scotia, and other nearby lands.

8. In the 18th century, the French and the British struggled for control of North America. The British took control of eastern Canada, and in 1755 sent between 6,000 -10,000 French-speaking Acadians out of the country. The Acadians (Cajuns) finally settled in Louisiana.

9. Mardi Gras is always 47 days before Easter. Easter is the first Sunday after the full moon on or after March 21. Easter can be as early as March 23 and as late as April 25.

10. Mardi Gras is the last day of "carnival," which is also celebrated in many other Catholic countries, especially the famous carnival in Rio de Janeiro, Brazil.

11. The Mardi Gras parade features floats, which are decorated vehicles with many people in costume riding on the vehicle. The first floats were used in 1837.

Kennedy Space Center page 91

1. The population of Florida (2000 census) is 15,982,378. It is the 4th largest state in population.

2. Cape Canaveral is on the Atlantic coast, about halfway between Florida's two largest cities. The largest city in population and area is Jacksonville, which is north of the Space Center.

3. Miami, south of Cape Canaveral, is home to large numbers of Cubans, Central Americans and Haitians. Miami is only 100 miles from Cuba.

4. Cape Canaveral was changed to Cape Kennedy in 1963 after the assassination of Kennedy. However, it was changed back to Cape Canaveral in 1973, and the space center was named the Kennedy Space Center.

5. The space shuttle is launched into orbit with rockets. It returns to earth in a long glide, like an airplane.

6. There are three main parts to the shuttle. The orbiter, the external tank, and the solid rocket boosters.

7. The first shuttle, *Enterprise*, was not launched. It was carried up by a 747 airplane and then released to practice landings.

8. The first launch of a shuttle was made in 1981. There were only two men in the crew.

9. The seventh flight carried the first woman astronaut, Sally Ride.

10. The seventeenth flight carried two monkeys and 24 rats.

11. The first shuttle disaster (*Challenger*) occured on January 28, 1986. It was the 25th shuttle mission. All seven crew members were killed less than two minutes after liftoff.

12. There are about 8,300 items the size of a baseball or larger orbiting the earth. Seven per cent are active satellites. The rest is space junk.

Castillo de San Marcos page 97

1. In the mid 16th century, the French and the Spanish came into conflict over the north Florida coastline. The French established Fort Caroline at Jacksonville.

2. A French fleet sailed south to fight the Spanish, but they were wrecked by a hurricane. The Spanish sailed north and destroyed Fort Caroline.

3. The Spanish returned and began a settlement at Saint Augustine. The Spanish captured the French at an island near St. Augustine. Most of the French men were killed because they refused to become Catholics (the French were Protestants). For that reason, the bay behind the island was called "Matanzas," which means "massacre" in English.

4. Saint Augustine is the oldest city in the U.S. It was built by the Spanish beginning in 1565.

5. The Spanish built a new fort in 1740 at Matanzas inlet. It served as a watchtower to warn Saint Augustine of any enemy.

6. In 1763, Britain took control of the fort as a result of the Treaty of Paris that ended the Seven Years War. The British named the fort, Fort St. Mark. The British made St. Augustine the capital of Eastern Florida

7. During the American Revolution, three signers of the Declaration of Independence were captured and put in prison at the fort.

8. The British made Pensacola the capital of Western Florida. During the Revolutionary War, The Battle of Pensacola was a long and hard battle, but the Spanish under Bernardo de Galvez defeated the British. Bernardo de Galvez was the only officer in the Revolutionary War who was never defeated.

9. When the U.S. took over the fort in 1821, they changed the name to Fort Marion. General Francis Marion was a hero of the Revolutionary War.

10. Some of the Seminole Indians of Florida were forced to move to Oklahoma. A few still live in southern Florida near Lake Okeechobee.

Washington, D.C. page 103

1. George Washington personally chose the site of the nation's capital in 1791.

2. The French architect and engineer Pierre Charles L'Enfant designed the city. Washington asked L'Enfant to do the design, but fired him after a year. The two men did not get along.

3. The population of Washington is 572,059, two-thirds of the population of the city is Black.

4. The Mall is a long stretch of grass and trees from the capitol to the Lincoln Memorial. The White House looks at the Washington Monument, which is on the mall.

5. The Potomac River forms the southwest boundary of the District of Columbia and Virginia. The Pentagon is across the river.

6. The National Air and Space Museum is the most visited museum in the world. Over 10 million people visit each year. Admission is free (it is free at all government memorials and museums). There are many historic aircraft in the museum.

7. The Jefferson Memorial is located on a pond called the Tidal Pool. Inside the Memorial there is a 19 foot statue of Jefferson. Although it is a beautiful memorial, it is less crowded than the other memorials.

8. Arlington National Cemetery is across the Potomac in Arlington, Virginia. It is the largest military cemetery in the U.S. There are over 240,000 graves. The Tomb of the Unknowns is a memorial that honors the unknown soldiers from America's wars.

9. The Korean War Veterans Memorial honors the veterans of the Korean War. It is located in southwest Washington. 54,246 Americans died in the Korean War.

10. The Franklin Delano Roosevelt Memorial honors the 32nd president of the U.S. Roosevelt served four terms. His terms include the end of the Great Economic Depression and World War II. The memorial has four parts, one for each of his terms. His wife, Eleanor Roosevelt, is also honored at the memorial.

Lincoln Memorial, Washington, D.C.

Kamehameha, first king of Hawaii

Also from Pro Lingua

Celebrating American Heroes by Anne Siebert

"This is a unique and wonderful book of 13 short plays in praise of American historical figures like Betsy Ross, Abraham Lincoln, Thomas Edison, Jackie Robinson, and the first astronauts to land on the moon. The tone of the plays is passionate – *they are exciting and fun but involve serious subjects* such as war, slavery, race relations, sacrifice, hard work, effort. The language isn't all "easy" – some of the main roles would be best for intermediate students or higher – but there is a special role for beginning students as part of the chorus.

"Like a 'Greek chorus,' this group speaks in unison and adds commentary to the action.... Everyone gets to participate in the play, even in a multi-level class. *You could think of these plays as 'Jazz Chants" but with cultural and historical content.* That is, all the students get to speak lines in loud, confident voices, which is good for pronunciation, intonation, and fluency. At the same time they are portraying and discussing meaningful issues from history.

"You don't have to be extremely brave to put on a play with your class. **The Teacher's Guide** *gives you short, clear instructions on how to proceed.* Students get to read their lines from the script, and the props can be very simple. We think these plays will bring a level of excitement into the classroom and give students the unforgettable feeling that they are participating in American history." *– review by* **Anna Silliman, *Hands-on English***

Heroes from American History by Anne Siebert

This companion volume to the playbook *Celebrating American Heroes* can be used with the plays or as an independent reader on American history that lends itself to serious cultural discussions and includes a variety of engaging activities: • reading and vocabulary development, • retelling, and • critical thinking and writing.

Plays for the Holidays by Anne Siebert

Help your students explore, understand, and take part in our American holidays. They're all here, the legal ones and many other favorites, from Labor Day at the beginning of the school year to Independence Day during the summer vacation. Most of the plays have historical subjects relating to the traditions and origins of the holidays. The students are carefully prepared for each play with a variety of activities explaining how the holidays are celebrated today and introducing the context of the story. Your students will enjoy and learn as they read, write, listen, and perform the plays.

For information or to order, visit our webstore at
www.ProLinguaAssociates.com
or call 800-366-4775
Pro Lingua Associates, P.O. Box 1348, Brattleboro, VT 05302

Bunker Hill Monument, Boston. MA